CAMBRIDGE

Macbeth

GCSE English Literature for AQA
Student Book

Anthony Partington and Richard Spencer
Series editor: Peter Thomas

CAMBRIDGE
UNIVERSITY PRESS

University Printing House, Cambridge CB2 8BS, United Kingdom

Cambridge University Press is part of the University of Cambridge.

It furthers the University's mission by disseminating knowledge in the pursuit of
education, learning and research at the highest international levels of excellence.

www.cambridge.org
Information on this title: www.cambridge.org/9781107453951 (Paperback)
www.cambridge.org/9781107453968 (Cambridge Elevate-enhanced Edition)
www.cambridge.org/9781107453975 (Paperback + Cambridge Elevate-enhanced Edition)

© Cambridge University Press 2015

First published 2015

Printed in Dubai by Oriental Press

A catalogue record for this publication is available from the British Library

ISBN 978-1-107-45395-1 Paperback
ISBN 978-1-107-45396-8 Cambridge Elevate-enhanced Edition
ISBN 978-1-107-45397-5 Paperback + Cambridge Elevate-enhanced Edition

Additional resources for this publication at www.cambridge.org/ukschools

....

Approval message from AQA

This textbook has been approved by AQA for use with our qualification. This means that we have checked that it broadly covers the specification and we are satisfied with the overall quality. Full details of our approval process can be found on our website.

We approve textbooks because we know how important it is for teachers and students to have the right resources to support their teaching and learning. However, the publisher is ultimately responsible for the editorial control and quality of this book.

Please note that when teaching the GCSE English Literature (8702) course, you must refer to AQA's specification as your definitive source of information. While this book has been written to match the specification, it cannot provide complete coverage of every aspect of the course.

A wide range of other useful resources can be found on the relevant subject pages of our website: aqa.org.uk

Contents

Introduction

Welcome to your AQA GCSE English Literature student book on *Macbeth* – one of Shakespeare's best-known plays, and one that we hope you will enjoy at GCSE and later in life. Some of the play deals with things you are familiar with, and may even be an expert on – ambition, conflicting loyalties, conscience, and decisions that affect your life and those around you.

This book will help you make the most of the play and of your GCSE. It will develop your skills in reading and responding to a Shakespeare text, and in writing for GCSE English Literature.

The book is organised as follows:

Part 1: Exploring the play
Part 1 leads you through each act of the play. It ensures you build an understanding of the action, dramatic structure and methods that Shakespeare uses to present his characters and ideas. Each unit provides activities for discussion and drama-based approaches.

You will also develop your skills in writing about the play. Your work in each unit will result in notes and focused responses on aspects of the play that are important for GCSE. These will also be useful when you revise for your exam.

Part 2: The play as a whole
Part 2 provides an overview of key aspects of the play, including structure, contexts, characterisation and language. It will develop your knowledge and understanding, and also help you to revise your responses to the play as a whole.

On Cambridge Elevate you will find video clips that deepen your experience, understanding, interpretations and analysis of the play.

Preparing for your exam
This part gives you practice and guidance to help you prepare for your examination. It also provides examples of answers showing skills at different levels, so you can assess where your skills are strong and where to focus your efforts to improve.

We hope that you will enjoy using these resources, not only to support your study, but to help you see that a Shakespeare play has plenty to say about the life around you – and within you.

Peter Thomas
Series editor

Introducing Macbeth

SHAKESPEARE AND *MACBETH*

Shakespeare's world

William Shakespeare was born in 1564 and died in 1616. This means that, as a boy, he would have been familiar with stories from old people about the execution of Sir Thomas More for treason in 1535, the Norfolk Rebellion of 1545, Thomas Wyatt's rebellion against Queen Mary and the burning of martyrs (including the Archbishop of Canterbury) as Catholics and Protestants used faith as an excuse for revenge.

During his own lifetime, he would have been familiar with further executions for treason or heresy, more rebellions, and the long reign of the second female monarch – Queen Elizabeth I. Add a few outbreaks of plague, public hangings for theft and an attempted invasion of England by the Spanish, and there was plenty of scope for a writer of tragedies, with comedies and romances as a welcome escape. In all, Shakespeare wrote 38 or 39 plays – many of which mix elements of comedy, tragedy, history and romance.

Macbeth

Macbeth was first performed in 1606, ten years before Shakespeare died, so it is the result of years of successful theatrical experience. He based the play on a popular work of history published by Raphael Holinshed in 1557, which described the life and times of the real Macbeth, who was born in 1005, became king of Scotland after killing King Duncan in battle in 1040, and who died in 1057.

The real King Duncan was recorded as a faithful Christian and a good ruler for 17 years, but few details are known about his life. Not that this mattered to Shakespeare – he was a dramatist, not a historian. He used the source material only as a basis for his story, adapting, developing or omitting details as he wanted in order to create a theatrical entertainment.

Structure and plot

The play contains five acts, each split into several scenes to vary the pace, mood, plot and characters. Not surprisingly, Act 1 establishes the main characters and the main action, Acts 2, 3, 4 develop the action and the characters, and Act 5 brings it all to a conclusion. The division into scenes keeps the audience engaged and interested, as Shakespeare changes the scene from castle to heath, from bedroom to banqueting hall, and from high tension to comedy.

 Read more about *Macbeth*'s structure and plot in Unit 6.

Context and setting

You need to know some context of Shakespeare's times, mainly about what theatres and audiences were like. This is not a history task. You simply need to know that Shakespeare wrote for an audience that was largely unable to read or write, as well as for those who were familiar with the stories that he was turning into plays. You need to know that the theatre he wrote for had none of the sound amplification, scenery, technical effects or lighting that we have today. He had to make use of an audience's imagination.

There are other contexts of performance – such as the different ways that a scene may be performed on screen and on stage, or for an audience of children or adults. However, the main contexts you need to know about are those of writing and performing. You are studying the play in the context of GCSE English Literature, which may be different from the context of watching it in the theatre.

 Read more about the context and setting of *Macbeth* in Unit 7.

Characterisation

Macbeth is a fine example of Shakespeare's skill in creating complex characters for an actor to perform. Macbeth himself, though a ruthless tyrant, does not begin as one, and it is his progress from royal servant to tyrant that charts the steps by which a good man may become bad. There are reminders along the way that some qualities remain which make an audience occasionally feel sympathy for a man who murders women and children, let alone a king. In other words, he makes Macbeth a realistic, multi-dimensional character. He uses soliloquies to show how Macbeth's thoughts and feelings are a mix of what most people think and feel.

Lady Macbeth is also realistically portrayed as a wife who backs her husband, understands him and motivates him when his resolution fails. This support comes at a great cost to her own state of mind. Other characters are presented largely as a contrast to Macbeth, including Duncan, Banquo and Macduff.

 Read more on characters and characterisation in *Macbeth* in Unit 8.

The ideas of the play

Themes are the subjects that drama can be based on. As in Shakespeare's day, the most common themes are love and hate in relationships, reactions to events large and small, and examples of human traits such as courage, doubts, fears, successes and failures.

Ideas are ways of understanding aspects of the themes. Ideas about love can be that love makes the world and people better, or that it makes them insecure and jealous, or that it does not last, or that it helps people through difficulty. Ideas about war are that it can bring out the best in people, or that it brings out the worst in people, that it is sadly necessary to defend something important or that it is tragic because it is not necessary.

Shakespeare did not write his play simply as entertainment. There were things he wanted to say and issues he wanted to explore. These are some of the ideas that you will find he returns to in the play:

- ambition
- appearance and reality
- evil
- tyranny and chaos.

 Read more about the themes and ideas in *Macbeth* in Unit 9.

Language

Shakespeare's greatest talent is his use of the English language. He writes speeches that convey a full range of passions and which realistically portray people from all walks of life – peasants, soldiers, lords and ladies, bishops, clowns and innkeepers. He uses imagery to create atmosphere and mood through words. In doing so, he helps his audience imagine things that cannot easily be shown on stage, relating them to ideas that would be familiar to those watching.

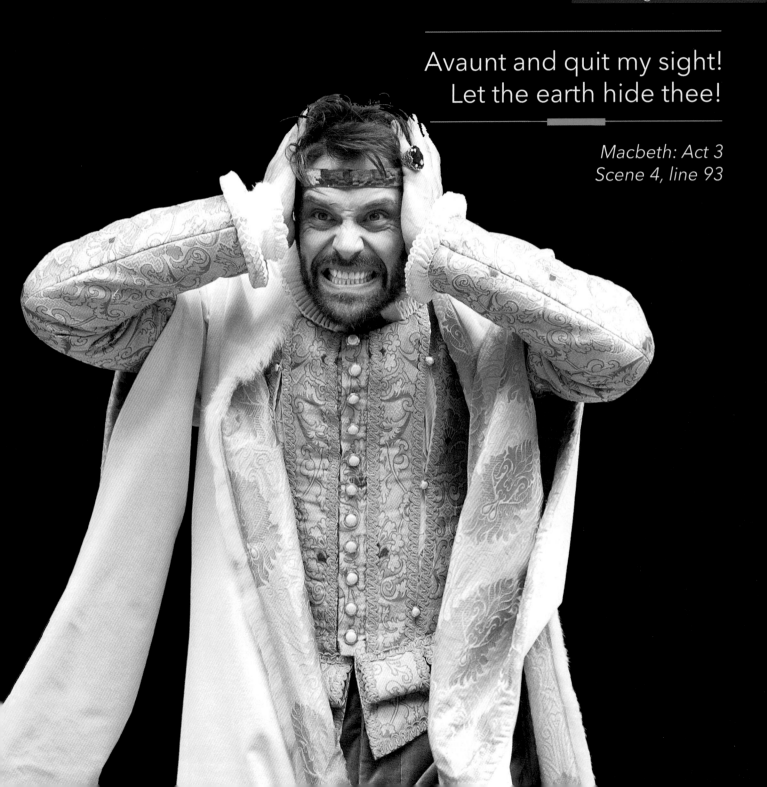

Avaunt and quit my sight!
Let the earth hide thee!

Macbeth: Act 3
Scene 4, line 93

For example when Banquo describes the darkness of the night by saying '**There's husbandry in heaven; / Their candles are all out.**' Shakespeare is drawing on the audience's knowledge of housekeeping (husbandry) and the simple fact that good housekeeping means saving money by putting out candles when they are not needed.

 Read more about language in *Macbeth* in Unit 10.

Interpretation and performance

Your own response to the play matters – what you think of the characters, which scenes make you laugh or think. Most important is what the play means to you when it shows you how people behave, and how relationships develop or go wrong. Interpretation can be personal to you, or related to all people, or to some people. For example some would see Macbeth as a foolish man to believe in prophecies, whereas others would see him as a man who had good reason to believe that the Witches were real, and trusted them more because one of their predictions soon came true.

Drama is public entertainment. Whether on stage or screen, or in your classroom, you will be getting closest to Shakespeare when you see the script turning into action. This is where your understanding of plot and character, themes and ideas, language, stagecraft and theatricality come together, because interpretation and performance are what the text is all about. Connecting the words with what actors have done with them, or with what you think actors could do with them, ensures that you write about Shakespeare as a dramatist.

There's husbandry in heaven;
Their candles are all out.

SHAKESPEARE AND GCSE ENGLISH LITERATURE

Your GCSE English Literature course has been designed so that you experience a range of drama, prose and poetry texts from the last few hundred years. The point of this range is that you understand that some things change over time – and some things do not. One of the most useful ways of exploring ideas in the play is to ask 'Is this about events and characters long gone, or is there something about them that you can still see today?' That question will lead you to the big issues of relevance, context and the value of Shakespeare as a writer.

Shakespeare in the exam

Your GCSE English Literature exam has two papers: Paper 1 is Shakespeare and the 19th-century novel, which is worth 40%, and Paper 2 is Modern texts and poetry, which is worth 60%.

Paper 1 is divided as follows:

Section A Shakespeare: this where you answer one question on your play of choice – *Macbeth* in this case. You will be required to write in detail about an extract from the play and then to write about the play as a whole.

Section B The 19th-century novel: this is where you answer one question on the novel of your choice. You will be required to write in detail about an extract from the novel and then to write about the novel as a whole.

GCSE English Literature assessment objectives

The GCSE English Literature assessment objectives form the basis for the GCSE mark scheme. You will be assessed on your skill in writing about what the play is about and how it is written. For Paper 1, Section A, you will be assessed on four AOs:

AO1: Read, understand and respond to texts. Students should be able to:

- maintain a critical style and develop an informed personal response
- use textual references, including quotations, to support and illustrate interpretations.

AO2: Analyse the language, form and structure used by a writer to create meanings and effects, using relevant subject terminology where appropriate.

AO3: Show understanding of the relationships between texts and the contexts in which they were written.

AO4: Use a range of vocabulary and sentence structures for clarity, purpose and effect, with accurate spelling and punctuation.

The 'contexts' of AO3 may also include the context in which a text is set, literary contexts such as genres, and the context of different audiences – including you in the 21st century.

LITERATURE SKILLS AND STUDY FOCUS AREAS

Most of your study will be based on reading the text, but this will not be enough if you are to understand and enjoy the play as drama. You need to realise that the text does not become drama until it is performed, and actors bring the words to life. So make sure that you see the play and connect the words on the page with performance on stage or screen.

Most of the skills you develop in your literature study will be the same as those in other parts of your GCSE English reading. You will develop your core skills to show understanding, interpretation and analysis. These skills, along with the following study focus areas, give a focus for your work in this book.

Ideas, attitudes and feelings

These amount to content. The important thing to remember is that they are three different things.

- **Ideas** are the thoughts that explain or result from an experience.
- **Attitudes** are the positions or postures adopted when facing experiences.
- **Feelings** are the emotions people feel, which are often quite different from their attitudes and ideas.

For example you could say that:

- An **idea** is that ambition can be a force for good or for ill.
- An **attitude** is that if you have gone so far, it is too difficult to go back, so you may as well go on.
- A **feeling** is pity that a potentially good man became so evil.

The writer's methods

You will be expected to understand and respond to the feelings, ideas or attitudes expressed in the play, and also understand and respond to the way the play is written – the writer's methods. These amount to language, form and structure, which are also three different things. For example you could say that:

- The **language** is written to help actors speak their lines and to convey ideas and feelings through imagery.
- The **form** is a five-act play with division into scenes.
- The **structure** is based on Macbeth's progress from loyal subject to ruthless tyrant.

Developing written response skills

This book supports you in writing that is focused on the GCSE study areas. It helps you to identify where your skills are strong and what you need to do to improve. Develop your skills from 'basic' comments that are relevant and include a quotation to support the comment, to using your understanding and interpretation skills to explain feelings, motives or reasons and to include ideas that develop and extend meaning. For example:

- **Shows a relevant response, supported with quotation:**
  It is about the way a man who was 'brave Macbeth' and 'worthy thane' becomes evil and ends up as 'this vile butcher'.
- **Shows understanding with clear explanation:**
  It is about a character who is influenced by his own 'vaulting' ambition and by some supernatural influence from 'the weird sisters' to kill a king he knows to be good in order to become king himself. He then realises that he has to keep killing to stay safe, and also that he was wrong to take the Witches' prophecies at face value.
- **Shows exploration and evaluation:**
  It is about Shakespeare's view of human beings as a mixture of good and evil, and what happens when the evil takes over. In Macbeth's case this is partly because of an internal motivation or a flaw of character – his ambition. Yet Shakespeare also shows that human beings can be vulnerable to external influences, some of them beyond normal human experience, such as the supernatural influence of the Witches. This presentation of a character and his destiny goes beyond the simple stereotype of people being totally good or evil.

Writing with focus

This book develops focused writing so you will be confident about writing in timed conditions in the exam. You need to show how Shakespeare builds the play as a theatrical experience to appeal to different people, using exciting stage effects. You also need to show how he uses characters as a mouthpiece for his ideas, and how he plays on audience sympathies, fears and suspense. When you respond to a question on the play you need to show that your response is dealing with essential skills, and linked to specific details of the text, making your points quickly and linking your chosen textual detail to a clear purpose.

THE ACTION OF MACBETH

Act 1

Three Witches gather in '**A desolate place**' and vow to meet with Macbeth after the battle he is fighting in is over.

Duncan, King of Scotland, is told by a wounded Captain that Macbeth and his friend, Banquo, fought bravely in the recent battle. As a reward, Duncan says he will promote Macbeth, giving him the defeated Thane of Cawdor's title.

Returning from battle, Macbeth and Banquo meet the Witches. They predict that Macbeth will be made Thane of Cawdor and, later, will become King of Scotland. They also predict that Banquo's son will one day be king. Macbeth shrugs off their predictions but reveals to the audience that he desires to be king. Immediately Ross arrives with news that Macbeth has indeed been made Thane of Cawdor.

Duncan welcomes Macbeth to his castle and formally makes him Thane of Cawdor. He declares that his own son, Malcolm, will one day succeed him as king.

At Macbeth's castle, Lady Macbeth receives a letter from her husband telling her about the Witches' prophecy. She wants her husband to be king and plots to murder Duncan, calling on evil spirits to help her. Macbeth arrives home and she promises to manage the killing.

Macbeth struggles with his conscience. Lady Macbeth accuses him of being a coward and says she will make it easy by poisoning Duncan's bodyguards. Macbeth agrees to murder the king.

Act 2

Macbeth returns from killing Duncan in an emotional state. He had tried to pray but found he could not say 'Amen'. Lady Macbeth has to return to the scene to frame the guards by covering their daggers with Duncan's blood. The Macbeths then go back to bed in order to appear innocent.

Macduff arrives to see Duncan. He finds the king's body and raises the alarm. Macbeth pretends to be horrified and kills the guard in a fake rage to cover his tracks. Duncan's sons, Malcolm and Donaldbain fear for their lives. They flee to England and Ireland respectively.

Act 3

Banquo suspects Macbeth of the murder. Remembering the Witches' prophecy that Banquo's sons will be kings, Macbeth hires Murderers to kill Banquo and his son Fleance. The murderers kill Banquo while he is hunting, but Fleance escapes.

During a feast, Macbeth sees Banquo's ghost. He reacts violently, surprising the other guests. Lady Macbeth reassures them. Macbeth vows to kill all his supposed enemies, starting with Macduff.

In a '*A desolate place*', Hecate, Goddess of the Witches, is angry that the Witches spoke with Macbeth without her permission. She promises to use magic to bring about his downfall.

In another part of Scotland, Lennox reveals that Malcolm, in exile in England, and Macduff plan to join forces to overthrow Macbeth.

Act 4

Macbeth visits the Witches again. Spirits warn that he should fear Macduff, but that nobody '**born of woman**' can harm him. He learns that he will be king until Birnam Wood comes to Dunsinane. Macbeth determines to kill Macduff, but is annoyed when the Witches confirm that Banquo's son will still be king.

Later Macbeth learns that Macduff has fled. Macbeth orders the killing of Macduff's family, which is brutally carried out.

In England, Malcolm tests Macduff's loyalty, then promises to be a good king. Ross arrives and informs Macduff that his wife and children have been killed. Malcolm is appalled at Macbeth's cruelty and Macduff vows to kill Macbeth himself.

Act 5

Sleepwalking and talking in her sleep, Lady Macbeth sees visions of blood on her hands. Her Doctor and Gentlewoman realise what she is guilty of.

The English army has marched on Scotland. Macbeth prepares for a siege, even though men are deserting him. He is furious that Malcolm is approaching. He is informed that Lady Macbeth cannot be cured. Later, Macbeth hears a scream and learns that his wife is dead.

Malcolm orders his army to disguise themselves using branches. Macbeth is shaken by the message he receives – he realises that Birnam Wood is coming to Dunsinane just as the Witches had predicted.

The battle begins and Macbeth fights fearlessly. No one is able to kill him. Finally, Macbeth comes face to face with Macduff. They fight and Macduff reveals that he was born by caesarian section – he is not '**of woman born**'. Macbeth's courage deserts him and Macduff kills him.

Macduff delivers Macbeth's head to Malcolm and hails him as the new king of Scotland. Malcolm invites all to attend his coronation.

THE MAIN CHARACTERS IN *MACBETH*

Macbeth begins the play as a wealthy and respected Scottish nobleman, the Thane of Glamis, who then murders his way to becoming king of Scotland.

Lady Macbeth is Macbeth's wife.

The Witches prophesise Macbeth's rise, sowing the seeds of his ambition to be king.

Duncan is the rightful King of Scotland who is murdered by Macbeth.

Banquo is a Scottish nobleman and a general in the king's army alongside Macbeth.

Macduff is the Thane of Fife, a Scottish nobleman of similar wealth and power to Macbeth.

Malcolm is Duncan's elder son and the rightful heir to the throne.

My thanes and kinsmen,
Henceforth be earls, the first
that ever Scotland
In such an honour named.

Malcolm: Act 5 Scene 9, lines 29–31

1

Act 1: Fair and foul

How does Shakespeare establish the play?

Your progress in this unit:
* understand and explain Shakespeare's choice for opening the play
* explore the way he establishes characters and ideas
* analyse Shakespeare's use of language and imagery
* develop a response to a writing task.

GETTING STARTED – THE PLAY AND YOU

Ambition – good or bad?

Ambition is a major **theme** in *Macbeth*. When is ambition a good thing? How can it be bad?

1 Work with a partner. Look at the following list. Which of these do you think are good ambitions? Which do you think might be unhealthy? Why? Discuss with a partner.

be rich
be the first person in my family to go to university
be successful
gain 6/8/10 GCSEs with top grades
get Grade 8 cello before I leave school

GETTING CLOSER – FOCUS ON DETAILS

Establishing the play

Act 1 in a play is mostly about 'establishing' important information for the audience. In Act 1 of *Macbeth*, Shakespeare establishes the plot, the atmosphere, the **characters** and the main ideas of the play. He grabs his audience's attention by his use of language and dramatic devices.

Read the summary of what happens in Act 1.

1 Using information from this summary, work in groups to discuss the key things that are 'established' in Act 1.

2 Write a five-line voiceover for a 'trailer' video for a new film of *Macbeth*. How will you make people want to go and see it? Use key words and short quotations that sum up the story.

Now read Act 1.

 Key terms

theme: an idea or concept that recurs throughout a play

Scene 1

The play opens dramatically with thunder and lightning. Three Witches plan to meet Macbeth.

Scene 2

A messenger tells King Duncan that the rebels have been defeated in battle. The Thane of Cawdor, who has betrayed the king, is executed. His title is given to Macbeth, and Macbeth and Banquo are both honoured for their bravery.

Scene 3

The Witches foretell that Macbeth will be Thane of Cawdor, then king. They also tell Banquo that his sons will be kings. Ross arrives and announces that Macbeth is now Thane of Cawdor. Macbeth starts to have '**horrible imaginings**' about being king.

Scene 4

Duncan honours Macbeth and Banquo, then names his son Malcolm as the next king. Macbeth expresses his '**black and deep desires**' to be king. Duncan plans to visit Macbeth in his castle.

Scene 5

Lady Macbeth reads a letter from Macbeth about the Witches' prophecy. When she learns that Duncan is to stay in their castle, she asks spirits to fill her with '**cruelty**'. When Macbeth arrives she tells him of her plans to murder the king.

Scene 6

King Duncan arrives at Macbeth's castle, which he says has a '**pleasant seat**'. Lady Macbeth greets him warmly. The king shows his trust in his hosts.

Scene 7

Macbeth struggles with the plan to kill Duncan, who is a guest in his house. Lady Macbeth persuades him not to be a '**coward**'. Macbeth agrees to do this '**terrible**' act.

Context: the wider picture

'**Context**' is a word you will often hear and read during your study of *Macbeth*. It refers to the things that are going on around a piece of literature. For a play like *Macbeth* these include:

- **the setting:** when and where it takes place and what was happening at the time. *Macbeth* is set in Scotland sometime around the 11th century.
- **how it was first performed:** *Macbeth* was written and first performed in London in about 1606, when public theatres (such as the Globe) were a new idea. The audience came from all walks of life.

 Find out what it was like to see *Macbeth* at the Globe theatre on Cambridge Elevate.

 Contexts

Macbeth was performed in front of the new king, James I, who was the patron of Shakespeare's acting company, The King's Men. James knew the story well, as it included his ancestors Banquo and Fleance. In addition to this, the king was very interested in witchcraft and had written a book about it. In retelling the story of the historical Macbeth, Shakespeare was flattering James as well as using an interesting tale for the purposes of his drama.

The supernatural atmosphere

Shakespeare's drama begins with the Witches. The '**foul**' setting creates a context where **supernatural** things can and do happen. The Witches' performance establishes a mood of threat and fear:

Fair is foul, and foul is fair,
Hover through the fog and filthy air.

Witches: Act 1 Scene 1, lines 12–13

1 Read Act 1 Scene 1.

   a What are the Witches planning to do?

   b How does Shakespeare suggest that the Witches know what is going to happen in the future? Identify lines or words that suggest this.

   c Notice how Shakespeare uses language to set the mood of this scene. List all the references to darkness and atmosphere you can find. Create a montage or mind map of any references you find using an image or colour scheme of your choice.

2 Look back at the summary of all the scenes in Act 1 at the beginning of this unit.

   a Why do you think Shakespeare chose to begin the play with the Witches rather than the entrance of King Duncan that begins Scene 2?

Fair is foul and foul is fair,
Hover through the fog and filthy air.

Witches: Act 1 Scene 1, lines 12–13

b What do the Witches add to the opening of the play?

c What would be the effect of removing this first scene?

3 Look at Act 1 Scene 3. Macbeth's opening line in the play is '**So foul and fair a day I have not seen**' (line 36). What might Macbeth mean by the words '**foul**' and '**fair**'? Decide which of the following statements is true. Give reasons for your answer.

a Macbeth is referring to the weather.

b Macbeth is referring to their recent success in the battle.

c Macbeth's comment is in reference to the light.

d Macbeth's meaning is unclear. Like the Witches, he is speaking in riddles.

 Watch actors discussing the meaning of this line on Cambridge Elevate.

4 The same words are used by the Witches in Scene 1. Why do you think Shakespeare transfers them to Macbeth in this scene?

5 Describe what the Witches promise Macbeth in Act 1 Scene 3. How does he react? Use quotations to support your answer.

6 Find either three video clips or three still images of Act 1 Scene 1 taken from different films or theatre productions. How does each one:

a establish the setting

b emphasise the supernatural

c create fear

d deliver the important lines about '**foul**'/'**fair**'?

Look carefully at:

- lighting
- staging (scenery and props)
- actors' movements and gestures
- sound effects.

Setting context in performance

The opening line gives any lighting designer or director a clue about what kind of atmosphere they should aim to create in a theatre. The line also carries a number of possible **connotations**. An actor playing Macbeth must decide which connotations are most important and consider how to show them. Remember that in the opening scene – unknown to Macbeth – the Witches are on stage and about to reveal themselves to him and Banquo for the first time.

Shakespeare's language in the first scenes may subtly hint at what is to come later in the play, particularly how Macbeth will believe the Witches' prophecies and be drawn into committing evil deeds.

1 What have you already heard or seen about Macbeth that could be described as either '**foul**' or '**fair**'?

2 Work in pairs or small groups to explore different ways of delivering aloud the '**foul and fair**' speech in Act 1 Scene 1, lines 12–13, or write a few lines of instruction or advice to an actor on how they might speak these lines in performance.

 Read more about the context and setting of *Macbeth* in Unit 7.

 Key terms

context: the historical circumstances of a piece of writing, which affect what an author wrote and the way they wrote it. Context also includes the way the writing was performed (in the case of plays such as *Macbeth*) and received by audiences.

supernatural: something that cannot be explained by the known laws of science and nature.

connotation: an idea or a feeling linked to the main meaning of a word – what it implies or suggests in addition to its literal meaning.

Establishing character relationships

Writers establish and develop characters in several ways, including through:

- **what they say** (their language, vocabulary and images)
- **what they do** (their actions, their reactions to events and their expressions of feeling)
- **how others respond to them or speak about them** (the language used to describe them and how people act or behave in their presence).

1 Shakespeare uses Act 1 to establish characters and their relationships. Copy and complete the following table to summarise what Shakespeare reveals about the central characters and how he engages the audience. Ask yourself the following questions:

a What do we know about the characters?
b What do we **want** to know?

Watch a video about King Duncan's character on Cambridge Elevate.

	The Witches	King Duncan	Macbeth	Lady Macbeth	Banquo
What do we know?					He is Macbeth's friend. He has a son. He stands in the way of Macbeth becoming king. According to the prophecy, his family will gain the throne.
What do we want to know?					How will his friendship with Macbeth change? Will Lady Macbeth kill him and his son? Is the Witches' prophecy true?

Macbeth's reputation

Following the noise of battle off stage, Act 1 Scenes 2 and 3 introduce Macbeth and establish him as a hero. Three characters praise Macbeth in his absence: the Captain, Duncan and Ross. He is admiringly reported to have been '**brave**' and '**noble**' in battle, compared to '**eagles**' and a '**lion**'.

1 Identify words or phrases used to describe Macbeth in Scene 2 that help to establish his reputation. How is he presented by others?

2 a Why do you think Shakespeare introduces us to Macbeth in this way?

b Which words or images from the Captain's description of Macbeth are most striking?

c What links can you find between the way Macbeth is described here at the start of the play and events later on? What do you later discover that Macbeth is capable of?

 Watch a video about how Macbeth's character is established on Cambridge Elevate.

Character and language

Look at how the Captain describes Macbeth:

For brave Macbeth – well he deserves that name –
Disdaining Fortune, with brandished steel,
Which smoked with bloody execution,
Like Valour's minion carved out his passage
Till he faced the slave,

Captain: Act 1 Scene 2, lines 16–20

1 What do these words make you think of? What connotations do they carry? Copy and complete the following table to record your answers.

Words used in relation to Macbeth	Associated words or connotations
'carve'	meat is carved; butchery; slaughter of people like animals
'Disdaining Fortune'	
'brandished steel'	
'smoked'	
'bloody execution'	
'valour'	

PUTTING DETAILS TO USE

Establishing Macbeth's character in Act 1

We find out a lot about Macbeth in Act 1, both from his own words and actions and from what other people say about him. This information helps us to build up a picture of the sort of man he is.

1 In the middle of a blank sheet of paper, write the question 'What do we find out about Macbeth in Act 1?'

Around this question, write down what you have found out about Macbeth's character during the first act of the play. Think about:

a what he says
b what he does
c how he reacts to what happens
d what other people say about him.

2 Work in small groups. Choose one person to take the role of an actor who is going to play Macbeth in a new production. They want to find out about their character at the start of the play. The other members of the group have just two minutes to coach 'Macbeth' and give him ideas. They must be based only on Act 1.

At the end of the two minutes, the actor should give a summary of what they have found out.

Macbeth and the witches

The Witches' prophecies in Act 1 Scene 3 fill Macbeth and Banquo with conflicting emotions.

1 How does Shakespeare make Macbeth and Banquo seem interested in what the Witches have to say?

2 What do you think is going through the minds of the two characters as they hear the prophecies? Write some 'thought bubbles' in modern English for:

a   Macbeth
b   Banquo.

3 Do you think the Witches are more dangerous or useful to Macbeth? Look at the ratings line and decide where you would place the Witches. Discuss your rating with a partner, giving reasons for your choice.

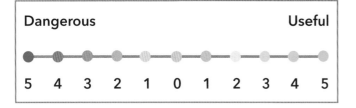

Dangerous									Useful
5	4	3	2	1	0	1	2	3	4	5

Macbeth and Lady Macbeth

In Act 1 Scene 2, the audience learns about aspects of Macbeth's character through the opinions of soldiers, lords and royalty. In Scenes 5–7, Shakespeare reveals aspects of Macbeth through the insight of the woman he lives with.

Lady Macbeth says that Macbeth is '**too full o'th'milk of human kindness**'. She shows her physical closeness to him by saying:

Your face, my thane, is as a book where men
May read strange matters.

Lady Macbeth: Act 1 Scene 5, lines 60–61

She also is seen to take control of events, instructing her husband how to behave and taking charge of the plans for Duncan's murder:

look like th'innocent flower,
But be the serpent under't.

Lady Macbeth: Act 1 Scene 5, lines 63–64

1 How well do you think Lady Macbeth knows her husband? Read Scene 5 and select three things she says about him that reveal important aspects of his character.

2 How does Lady Macbeth seem to control her husband? Identify any commands or instructions that she gives him.

Your face, my thane, is as a book where men May read strange matters.

Lady Macbeth: Act 1 Scene 5, lines 60–61

Learning checkpoint

How do you think Shakespeare wants you to view Macbeth's character in the play so far?

1 Create a table like the one shown to investigate statements A-E.

A At the start of the play, Macbeth is a warm, friendly character with many good qualities.

B At the start of the play, Macbeth is already a murderous and dark figure whom we dislike.

C At the start of the play, Macbeth is shown to be capable of violence and cruelty but also to be much admired and respected.

D The Witches poison Macbeth's character and mind with evil suggestions.

E The Witches merely exploit Macbeth's own ambition and cruelty.

	Strongly Agree	Agree	Disagree	Strongly Disagree
A At the start of the play, Macbeth is a warm, friendly character with many good qualities.	☐	☐	☐	☐
Supporting quotations:				
B At the start of the play, Macbeth is already a murderous and dark figure whom we dislike.	☐	☐	☐	☐
Supporting quotations:				

a After thinking about these statements or discussing them with others, decide the extent to which you agree with them.

b Find evidence in the form of quotations to support the statements. Which line or quotation would you use to prove or defend what you think about Macbeth's character?

c Add your own original statements describing how you think Shakespeare wants you to feel about Macbeth in the opening three scenes. Provide evidence to support them.

 Fill in the table on Cambridge Elevate.

3 Shakespeare uses **soliloquy** to allow the audience to hear the thoughts of characters directly. Alone on stage in Act 1 Scene 7 (lines 1–28), Macbeth struggles with his conscience as he plots to kill King Duncan:

> He's here in double trust:
> First, as I am his kinsman and his subject,
> Strong both against the deed; then, as his host,
> Who should against the murderer shut the door,
> Not bear the knife myself.

Macbeth: Act 1 Scene 7, lines 12–16

> **Key terms**
>
> **soliloquy:** a long speech given by a character, usually alone on stage, as if they are thinking aloud.

a What reasons does Macbeth give as to why Duncan should trust him?

b List five reasons why Macbeth should be afraid of killing Duncan.

c List the reasons why you think he has to go ahead with the murder.

4 When his wife enters, Macbeth tells her that he '**will proceed no further in this business**' (line 31).

Read through lines 35–59 in Act 1 Scene 7.

a How does Lady Macbeth persuade her husband to go ahead with the murder?

b What does she accuse him of? Why does she think this will make him change his mind?

Explore two different interpretations of Act 1 Scene 7 on Cambridge Elevate.

 Read more on characters and characterisation in *Macbeth* in Unit 8.

Who should against the murderer shut the door, Not bear the knife myself.

Macbeth: Act 1 Scene 7, lines 15–16

GETTING IT INTO WRITING

Writing about Shakespeare's presentation of Macbeth

Complete this assignment on Cambridge Elevate.

1 Drawing together the progress you have made in this unit, write a response to the following question:

How does Shakespeare present the character of Macbeth in Act 1?

You should write about:

a how Shakespeare develops Macbeth's character in Act 1
b how the Witches' prophecies and Lady Macbeth influence Macbeth.
c Whether Shakespeare encourages any sympathy or admiration for Macbeth.

Use some of the following prompts to help structure your response.

This is clear when he says …

For example the word … implies …

We can tell that he feels … by …

He explores the idea of …

When the audience hears him say …

Macbeth shares feelings of …

The line … suggests …

For example the audience can tell that …

It is obvious that he wants …

His language is full of …

An audience would feel …

Lady Macbeth's response suggests …

Learning checkpoint

When writing about 'how Shakespeare presents' you will need to consider how a character is shown to think and behave at various times in the play. Macbeth, for example, behaves and speaks very differently at the opening of the play and at the end of Act 1. You will also need to show that you understand how the character is presented through the language that they use.

How will I know I've done this well?

✔ **The best answers** will explore why Shakespeare wanted to show different sides to a character, and analyse the way he uses language to make his audience think and feel. They offer a personal response and include supportive detail from the text.

✔ **Good answers** will explain how Shakespeare has made the characters interesting and believable, and ensured that what happens is interesting to watch. They will include references to well-chosen examples.

✔ **Weaker answers** will describe a character as a real person and what happens in the play as if it was true. It will not include many examples or mention what Shakespeare does as a writer.

GETTING FURTHER

Investigating soliloquy

 1 Compare Shakespeare's use of soliloquy in Act 1 Scene 7 with the following. What does each soliloquy tell us about Macbeth?

a Macbeth's soliloquy in Act 1 Scene 3, where he reflects on the Witches' prophecies

b Lady Macbeth's soliloquy in Act 1 Scene 5, lines 13–28, where she shows how well she understands Macbeth.

2 List all the soliloquies in Act 1, then identify the purpose of each one. Is it meant to:

a reveal how a character responds to what has happened (**characterisation**)

b reveal what a character is going to do

c reveal private thoughts and feelings that are overheard by another character on stage (**dramatic irony**).

Key terms

characterisation: the way a writer paints a picture of a particular character, through their words, actions and reactions.

dramatic irony: when the audience knows something that the characters on stage are unaware of.

Shakespeare in performance: stagecraft and theatricality

'Stagecraft' refers to the ways in which actors, directors and designers use the stage for maximum effect. Exploring stagecraft means analysing the use of space, props, costumes and technical elements to enhance the drama.

 1 Look at the quotations opposite. Write a short comment on the way that each one offers an opportunity for great drama on stage. Think about these questions:

a What stagecraft does Shakespeare encourage in order to create a dark and thrilling atmosphere?

b What does each of the quotations suggest could happen on stage?

c What challenges or opportunities do they present to a director?

Connect to the text

When you are writing about the dramatic or theatrical effect of a scene or moment, look for the clues in the text and include them in your answer.

In Act 1 Scene 3, for example, the audience knows that Macbeth's arrival is signalled by a drum because the Witch says '**A drum, a drum; Macbeth doth come**'. The rhyme in this line suggests the beating of a drum and gives a clue as to how Shakespeare wanted the drum beat to sound.

Stars, hide your fires, Let not light see my black and deep desires

Macbeth: Act 1 Scene 4, lines 50–51

What bloody man is that?

(of the Captain) Duncan: Act 1 Scene 2, line 1

Here I have a pilot's thumb,
Wrecked as homeward he did come.

First Witch: Act 1 Scene 3, lines 26-27

they meant to bathe in reeking wounds

(of Macbeth and Banquo) Captain: Act 1
Scene 2, line 39

A drum, a drum;
Macbeth doth come.

Third Witch: Act 1 Scene 3, lines 28-29

But I am faint, my gashes cry for help.

Captain: Act 1 Scene 2, line 42

What are these,
So withered and so wild in their attire,
that look not like th'inhabitants o'th'earth

Banquo: Act 1 Scene 3, lines 37-39

Thunder. Enter the three Witches

Stage direction: Act 1 Scene 3

Witches vanish.

Banquo: … whither are they vanished?
Macbeth: Into the air, and what seemed
   corporal,
Melted as breath into the wind.

Act 1 Scene 3 lines 78-80

First Witch: Where hast thou been sister?
Second Witch: Killing swine

Witches: Act 1 Scene 3, lines 1-2

Stars, hide your fires,
Let not light see my black and deep desires

Macbeth: Act 1 Scene 4, lines 50-51

2

Act 2: Alarms and escapes

How do the action and the characters develop?

Your progress in this unit:
- explore the motives and relationship of Macbeth and Lady Macbeth
- consider the possible ways of interpreting the text in performance
- explore Shakespeare's use of language and imagery
- learn how to write good answers.

GETTING STARTED - THE PLAY AND YOU

What is tragedy?

Macbeth is described as a **tragedy** - a form of drama with its origins in ancient Greece. The word tragedy is also used to describe terrible events, particularly those that involve death and disaster.

1 Look up the different meanings of 'tragedy' in a dictionary.

2 The word 'tragedy' is often used in news reporting. Find a recent news event that you would describe as a tragedy. Discuss these as a class.

3 Why do you think *Macbeth* is called a tragedy?

Key terms

tragedy: a play with an unhappy ending, usually involving the downfall of the main character.

GETTING CLOSER - FOCUS ON DETAILS

Developing the action

Act 2 of *Macbeth* is in four scenes. Shakespeare shows us Macbeth's disturbed state of mind before and after he murders Duncan, and how Lady Macbeth responds to this. The language of this act is full of images of violence and horror, and we hear of events that seem to go against nature. The atmosphere is one of danger and suspicion.

Read the following summary of what happens in Act 2, and then read Act 2.

Scene 1
Macbeth hallucinates about seeing a blood-stained dagger pointing the way to Duncan's bedroom. His mind is filled with images of horror.

Scene 2
Macbeth is shocked and frightened after killing Duncan. Lady Macbeth returns the daggers to the scene of the crime to frame the guards by covering them with Duncan's blood. They return to bed in order to appear innocent.

Scene 3
Macduff finds the murdered king's body and raises the alarm. Macbeth kills the king's guards in a false show of rage. Lady Macbeth faints. Duncan's sons, Malcolm and Donaldbain, fear there is a plot against them and escape to England and Ireland respectively.

Scene 4
A Scottish nobleman, Ross, discusses recent unnatural events with an old man. Macduff tells them that Macbeth has been made king, but says he will not attend the coronation.

1 Read lines 1–9 of Act 2 Scene 1. How does Shakespeare set the scene at the beginning of this act? What do these opening lines reveal about the scene?

2 Read the Porter's speech at the beginning of Act 2 Scene 3.

a Some productions omit this speech completely. What reasons can you think of for including it? It might help you to consider:
- where the speech comes in the play
- the mood of the speech
- the things that the Porter says.

b Read the speech carefully. How do the references and images relate to the key **themes** of the play?

Macbeth's state of mind

In Act 1, Macbeth was clearly nervous about the idea of killing Duncan. As Act 2 progresses, we find out that Macbeth is indeed capable of murder. However, he is also haunted by what he has done and by his own conscience.

1 Read lines 33–49 from Macbeth's **soliloquy** in Act 2 Scene 1.

a Describe in your own words what Macbeth sees.
b How does he explain it?

 Watch a video about atmosphere in language on Cambridge Elevate.

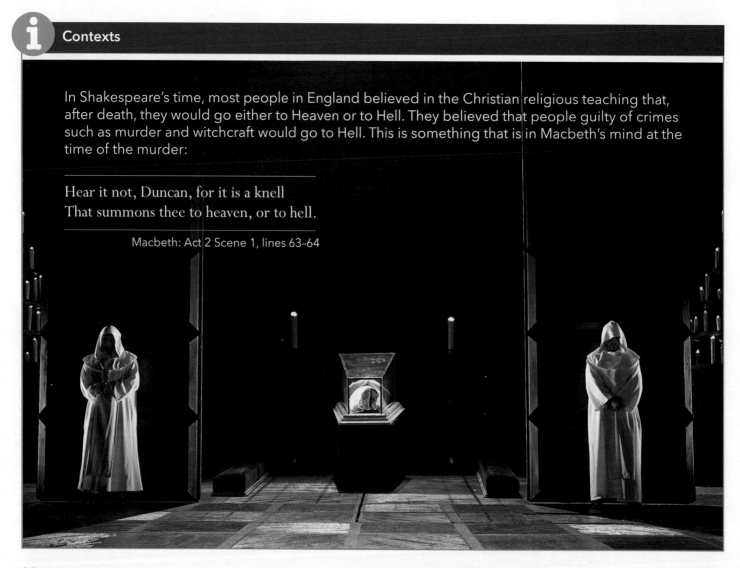

> **Contexts**
>
> In Shakespeare's time, most people in England believed in the Christian religious teaching that, after death, they would go either to Heaven or to Hell. They believed that people guilty of crimes such as murder and witchcraft would go to Hell. This is something that is in Macbeth's mind at the time of the murder:
>
> Hear it not, Duncan, for it is a knell
> That summons thee to heaven, or to hell.
>
> Macbeth: Act 2 Scene 1, lines 63–64

2 In the second part of this speech, Macbeth's mind is full of images of evil.

a List key words from lines 49–64 that help create these images.

b In pairs, discuss what images come into your mind as you read the second part of this soliloquy.

3 Look at the following things that Macbeth says to Lady Macbeth in Act 2 Scene 2, just after he has murdered Duncan:

I have done the deed. (line 14)

This is a sorry sight. (line 23)

I could not say 'Amen' (line 31)

Macbeth shall sleep no more. (line 46)

I am afraid to think what I have done (line 54)

How is't with me when every noise appals me? (line 61)

Wake Duncan with thy knocking: I would thou couldst. (line 77)

What do these comments suggest about his state of mind at this point in the play? Write some brief notes to **describe** in your own

words how you think he is feeling. You may find some of the following words helpful:

anxious	conflicted	haunted
terrified	determined	doubting
appalled	influenced	excited
trepidatious	cowardly	worried

4 Complete the following statements to show your interpretation of Macbeth's thoughts and feelings. Remember, for this activity you need to do more than just describe how Macbeth is feeling. You are being asked to:

- show how these feelings are suggested in the **language** he uses
- explain how an actor might show these feelings in performance.

a After he murders King Duncan, Macbeth is left feeling … .

b The language Macbeth uses suggests that he is … .

c Macbeth appears to be … .

d An actor might portray Macbeth in this scene by … .

 Read more about language in *Macbeth* in Unit 10.

I am afraid to think what I have done

Macbeth: Act 2 Scene 2, line 54

PUTTING DETAILS TO USE

Lady Macbeth's motives

Lady Macbeth is a strong-willed character. She is ambitious and determined. These can be positive qualities – they do not usually turn people into murderers! To find out what Lady Macbeth's motives might be for murder, you need to explore further.

1 Look at the following table, which gives one possible motive for Lady Macbeth's actions and provides evidence to support the idea.

Motive	How do we know?	Evidence from the text
She thinks the crown is the most valuable thing a person can possess.	She questions Macbeth's courage and reminds him of the power of the crown in Act 1 Scene 7.	'Wouldst thou have that / Which thou esteem'st the ornament of life, / And live a coward in thine own esteem'

Using Acts 1 and 2, think of two or three other possible motives that might drive Lady Macbeth to murder Duncan. Add your ideas and supporting evidence to a copy of the table.

2 Re-read Act 2 Scene 2. Find an example of Lady Macbeth's actions that show her strong will and determination. Then find a quotation from the text to back up your point.

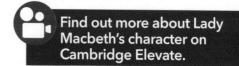
Find out more about Lady Macbeth's character on Cambridge Elevate.

Wouldst thou have that Which thou esteem'st the ornament of life ...

Lady Macbeth: Act 1 Scene 7, lines 41–42

How does Lady Macbeth influence her husband?

Look at this grid showing some of the ways that Lady Macbeth influences Macbeth (or helps to control events by her own actions) in Acts 1 and 2.

Advises Macbeth not to dwell on thoughts of guilt.

Reminds Macbeth of the Witches' prophecy.

Offers to make all the arrangements for Duncan's murder.

Commands Macbeth to wash the blood off his hands and smear it on the guards to frame them.

Summons evil spirits to give her the strength to help kill Duncan.

Advises Macbeth to be deceitful and to look innocent in front of others.

Smears the guards with blood instead of Macbeth because he is too afraid to return to the scene of the crime.

Plays the hostess, welcoming and flattering Duncan to put him at ease.

Questions Macbeth's bravery and accuses him of cowardice when he suggests not killing Duncan.

Faints or pretends to faint when Duncan's body is found.

Reminds Macbeth that she has borne children and would rather kill them than go back on a promise.

Encourages Macbeth to be brave and to stick to the plan. She reassures him they will succeed.

1 Make a table with three columns: 'Actions', 'Influences' and 'Evidence'.

a   List each of the statements from the grid in the appropriate column.

b   In the 'Evidence' column, find short quotations from Acts 1 and 2 to support each of these ideas.

2 Using your quotations, make a mind map of words and phrases that Lady Macbeth uses that show:

a   her ability to persuade Macbeth to do what she wants

b   her determination and strength

c   her own actions.

'But screw your courage to the sticking-place and we'll not fail'.

Lady M's influence

Interpreting the evidence

Act 2 Scene 2 is the point in the play when Lady Macbeth is at her most powerful and active. Here, she plays an important part in Duncan's murder. You have already explored her behaviour and actions. Now you need to identify precisely what she says and does to influence or shape your opinion of her.

1 Look at the following quotations from Lady Macbeth in Act 2 Scene 2. For each of them:

a   identify any words or phrases you find significant or interesting
b   explain how what she says affects Macbeth and his actions.

The first has been completed for you as an example.

>   Go get some water
> And wash this filthy witness from your hand.
> Why did you bring these daggers from the place?
> They must lie there. Go carry them and smear
> The sleepy grooms with blood.

Lady Macbeth: Act 2 Scene 2, lines 49–53

The phrase 'filthy witness' draws the audience's attention to Macbeth's blood-stained hands. The word 'witness' connotes a crime and reminds us of their guilt. She gives Macbeth two different commands to 'Go' in a short space of time. This suggests both the tension and confusion that she is feeling and the control she has over him.

Learning checkpoint

How will I know I've done this well?

✔ You will have explained why and how her words make her powerful.

✔ You will have identified how she influences Macbeth.

✔ You will have used interpreting phrases such as 'this suggests' or 'this implies' to show how an audience responds to her words.

✔ You will have used key terminology, ensuring accurate spelling and clear, well-punctuated sentences.

Hark, peace!
It was the owl that shrieked, the fatal bellman
Which gives the stern'st good-night. He is about it.
The doors are open, and the surfeited grooms
Do mock their charge with snores. I have drugged their possets,
That death and nature do contend about them,
Whether they live, or die.

Lady Macbeth: Act 2 Scene 2, lines 3-8

Infirm of purpose!
Give me the daggers. The sleeping and the dead
Are but as pictures; 'tis the eye of childhood
That fears a painted devil. If he do bleed,
I'll gild the faces of the grooms withal,
For it must seem their guilt.

Lady Macbeth: Act 2 Scene 2, lines 55-59

My hands are of your colour, but I shame
To wear a heart so white.
Knock [within]
I hear a knocking
At the south entry. Retire we to our chamber;
A little water clears us of this deed.
How easy is it then!

Lady Macbeth: Act 2 Scene 2, lines 67-71

Putting Lady Macbeth on trial

1 Imagine that Lady Macbeth is being put on trial for her part in Duncan's murder. Split the class into two groups: one for the defence and one for the prosecution.

a   Prepare by gathering and discussing the evidence from the first two acts of the play. Then make a list of key points to support your case.

b   Appoint someone to present your case to the judge (your teacher). Everyone in the group should join in the discussion.

c   When you are ready, present your case.

d   What is the verdict?

 Watch a speech for the prosecution on Cambridge Elevate.

 Watch a speech for the defence on Cambridge Elevate.

 Learning checkpoint

An important part of exploring any **character** is to consider what other characters say about them. Think about what other characters say about Lady Macbeth. In Act 2 Scene 3, for example, Macduff refers to her as '**gentle lady**' (line 77). The use of this **adjective** may surprise you: the audience has just witnessed her with blood-covered hands! In fact, 'gentle lady' refers to Lady Macbeth's social class rather than her personality. It recalls Duncan calling Macbeth '**gentleman**' in Act 1 Scene 2. Using the word 'gentle' reminds the audience of Lady Macbeth's status and her relationship with the king (which she has just betrayed).

1 List 10 adjectives you would choose to describe Lady Macbeth. You might use a spider diagram to do this, writing the title 'What is Lady M like?' in the middle of a blank sheet, and writing the words around it.

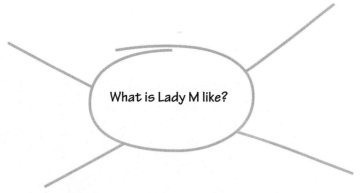

What is Lady M like?

2 Make a list of the things others say about Lady Macbeth in Acts 1 and 2. What do they tell us about her?

3 Compare your lists from Questions 1 and 2. How are they different? Why do you think this is?

Imagery in Act 2

After Macbeth kills Duncan, his language is full of doubt and regret. He seems obsessed with the idea that he has sealed his fate and that he will pay a heavy price for his actions. In Act 2, Shakespeare frequently uses **imagery** about sleep:

Still it cried, 'Sleep no more' to all the house;
'Glamis hath murdered sleep', and therefore Cawdor
Shall sleep no more: Macbeth shall sleep no more.

Macbeth: Act 2 Scene 2, lines 44–46

1 Why do you think Macbeth is so obsessed by the idea of not sleeping again? How do lines 44–46 help you to interpret his state of mind in Act 2 Scene 2?

2 Shakespeare (through Macbeth) makes constant reference to sleep in this scene, often through the use of imagery. Make a list of all the references to sleep in this scene. Choose two or three of these references. For each one, write a paragraph to explain:

a the image created by the language, and what it means
b the **connotations** of the imagery.

Here is an example:

When Macbeth refers to sleep as the 'balm of hurt minds' it implies that he is experiencing mental pain and that he fears he will never again receive the 'balm' or relief that sleep provides. This imagery reflects the anguish and doubt he is feeling and is an expression of his guilt.

Key terms

adjective: a word that describes a noun.

imagery: language intended to conjure up a vivid picture in the reader or audience's mind.

Macbeth shall sleep no more.

Macbeth: Act 2 Scene 2, line 46

GETTING IT INTO WRITING

Writing about Macbeth

1 Drawing together the progress you have made in this unit, write an extended answer to one of the following questions. Your response should be no longer than 300 words.

How does Shakespeare establish and present the character of Macbeth as the 'hero' in the early part of the play?

How does Shakespeare present Macbeth's actions and feelings around the murder of King Duncan?

Connect to the text

You should always try to make specific, detailed connections when using quotations. Do not just explain what they mean – try to show what the quotation suggests or implies about a character, theme or idea.

When writing about **characterisation**, you should remember to explore how a character is presented through:

- the language that they use – what they **say**
- their actions – what they **do**.

Learning checkpoint

How will I know I've done this well?

✔ **The best answers** will explore what Shakespeare does to create character. They offer a personal response and provide many well-explained details.

✔ **Good answers** will show a clear understanding of what Shakespeare does to create character using well-chosen examples.

✔ **Weaker answers** will only explain what happens to a character without using many examples or mentioning what Shakespeare does as a writer.

Complete this assignment on Cambridge Elevate.

I'll go no more.
I am afraid to think what I have done;
Look on't again, I dare not.

Macbeth: Act 2 Scene 2, lines 54–56

> Lady Macbeth: Did you not speak?
> Macbeth: When?
> Lady Macbeth: Now.
> Macbeth: As I descended?

Act 2 Scene 2, lines 16-19

GETTING FURTHER

Speaking Shakespeare: the clues are in the lines

You might think it is difficult to speak Shakespeare's lines. In fact, the way the lines are written gives lots of helpful clues about how they should be spoken.

Look closely at Act 2 Scene 2, lines 14–46. The lines alternate quickly between Macbeth and Lady Macbeth, and Macbeth's lines are broken up with lots of punctuation. The rhythm and speed of these short lines reflects the tension and excitement in the scene. This rapid delivery of lines is a technique called **stichomythia**.

1 What is the effect of the stichomythia in Act 2 Scene 2? How does it reflect and enhance the dramatic action?

2 Find another example from Act 2 where punctuation and/or line length give clues to how the actor should deliver the lines. Try speaking the lines yourself. How do the clues in the text help you?

3 Find other examples from Act 2 where the line structure or punctuation helps to create a particular tone or mood – for example excitement, stillness or nervousness.

Imagery

In *Macbeth*, Shakespeare uses language to create powerful imagery of good and evil, heaven and hell, sleep and death, night and day.

1 Find an example of imagery from each scene of Act 2 that you think is especially memorable. Write a brief commentary about each example. Consider:

a how Shakespeare uses language to create the image for the audience
b key words and phrases
c the effect of the image – its dramatic effect, the atmosphere it creates or what it reveals about a character.

🔑 Key terms

stichomythia: the use of short, quick alternate lines in dialogue between two characters.

3

Act 3: Illusions and delusions

How is evil presented in *Macbeth*?

Your progress in this unit:
- interpret the role of the Witches in the play
- understand the ways evil is presented and the importance of the supernatural in the play
- analyse Macbeth's tyrannical actions and his use of dark and violent language
- develop written response skills.

GETTING STARTED – THE PLAY AND YOU

What makes a tyrant?

In the last scene of Act 3, Lennox twice refers to Macbeth as a '**tyrant**'. A tyrant is a leader who rules by fear, not allowing any opposition or free speech. Tyrants often create division between different groups and individuals in order to remove rivals and destroy enemies.

1 Work with a partner. Write a list of real people in history who could be called tyrants.

2 Talk together about what you think it would be like to live in a country or state ruled by a tyrant.

GETTING CLOSER – FOCUS ON DETAILS

The influence of evil

Act 3 begins just after Macbeth has become king. It details his development from an ambitious, murdering thane to a tyrant king. This act features a number of **supernatural** events, most famously Macbeth's sighting of Banquo's blood-soaked ghost at the feast.

Read the summary of what happens in Act 3.

1 Each of the following quotations is taken from one of the six scenes in Act 3.

a Macbeth: Thou canst not say I did it; never shake / Thy gory locks at me!

b Lennox: Fly to the court of England and unfold / His message ere he come, that a swift blessing / May soon return to this our suffering country / Under a hand accursed.

c Lady Macbeth: Things without all remedy / Should be without regard; what's done, is done.

d Banquo: O, treachery! / Fly, good Fleance, fly, fly, fly!

e Hecate: Get you gone / And at the pit of Acheron / Meet me i'th'morning. Thither he / Will come to know his destiny.

f Banquo: Thou hast it now, King, Cawdor, Glamis, all, / As the weïrd women promised, and I fear / Thou played most foully for't.

Use the summary of the scenes to help you decide which quotation comes from which scene in Act 3, and then read Act 3.

Scene 1

Banquo suspects that Macbeth murdered Duncan. Macbeth invites Banquo to his feast as guest of honour. Remembering the Witches' prophecy that Banquo's sons will be kings, Macbeth meets with two hired murderers and persuades them to kill Banquo and Banquo's son, Fleance.

Scene 2

Macbeth shares with Lady Macbeth his feelings of guilt and fear at the terrible deeds he has done, and what he knows is going to happen to Banquo.

Scene 3

Three Murderers kill Banquo while he is hunting, but Fleance escapes.

Scene 4

Macbeth is troubled by the news of Fleance's escape. He sees the ghost of Banquo sitting at the table during the feast. The guests are startled by Macbeth's strange and violent behaviour, but Lady Macbeth reassures them that he is fine. When the guests have left, Macbeth vows to kill all who oppose him, starting with Macduff. He decides to visit the Witches again to find out his fate.

Scene 5

The goddess Hecate is angry with the Witches for what they have said to Macbeth. She promises to use magic to bring down the over-confident and wicked Macbeth.

Scene 6

Lennox, one of the Scottish lords, reveals that Malcolm – in exile in England – and Macduff plan to join forces to overthrow Macbeth.

2 Explain what each quotation tells you about what happens in Act 3. Record your answers in a table like this. The first one has been done for you as an example.

Order.	Quote (including scene and line numbers)	What does this tell us about what happens in Act 3?
1f	'Banquo: Thou hast it now, King, Cawdor, Glamis, all, / As the weïrd women promised, and I fear / Thou played most foully for't.' (Act 3 Scene 1, lines 1–3)	Banquo reminds the audience that everything the Witches predicted in Act 1 has come true. He also expresses his own private suspicion that Macbeth did wicked things to enable him to become king.

Macbeth and the Murderers

Macbeth kills Duncan with his own hands, but in Acts 3 and 4 he avoids personally carrying out further murders. Instead, he arranges for the killing to be done by others. In Act 3 Scene 1, Macbeth persuades two Murderers to kill Banquo. He does this by making them feel that they have a grudge against Banquo and therefore a reason to kill him:

Know, that it was he in times past which held you so under fortune, which you thought had been our innocent self.

Macbeth: Act 3 Scene 1, lines 78–79

1 Look at Act 3 Scene 1, lines 91–107. In this speech, Macbeth taunts the Murderers.

    a What comparison does he make?
    b How might this persuade the Murderers?

2 Look at the image of Macbeth and the Murderers below. This Macbeth stands over them, suggesting he is superior to them. What language suggests this as an interpretation?

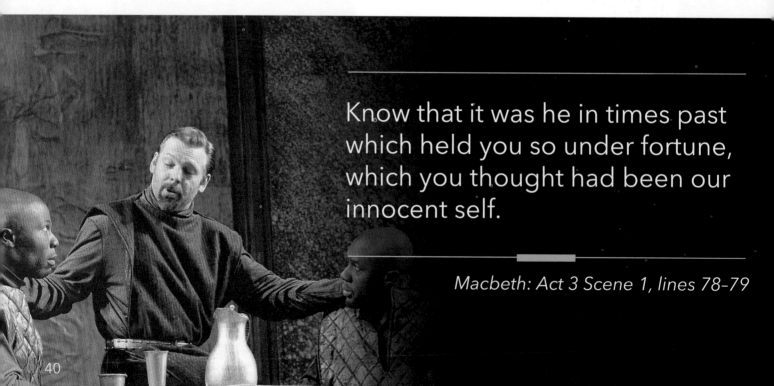

Know that it was he in times past which held you so under fortune, which you thought had been our innocent self.

Macbeth: Act 3 Scene 1, lines 78–79

Macbeth's dark thoughts

Shakespeare traces Macbeth's journey to evil through his language, which becomes darker and more disturbing as the play progresses. Act 3 Scene 2 represents a turning point. We see how Lady Macbeth grows concerned about her husband's state of mind. She asks him:

How now, my lord, why do you keep alone,
Of sorriest fancies your companions making
Using those thoughts which should have indeed died
With them they think on?

Lady Macbeth: Act 3 Scene 2, lines 8–11

When talking to the Murderers in Scene 1, Macbeth seemed confident. Now this confidence has been undermined by 'sorriest fancies' (miserable visions).

1. Read Macbeth's response to Lady Macbeth (Act 3 Scene 2, lines 13–26). Make a list of all the words that suggest fear, evil and darkness.

2. What does the language in this speech suggest about Macbeth's state of mind?

3. Look at the examples of imagery in Act 3 Scene 2, then copy and complete the table below to explain:

   a. their literal meaning
   b. how they can be interpreted
   c. the effect they may have on the audience.

   The first one has been completed for you as an example.

4. Look at Act 3 Scene 2, lines 46–53. Here, Macbeth seems to wrestle with disturbing images of day and night. These represent the conflict that is taking place in his mind.

   a. Identify the references to day and night in this speech.
   b. What distinction between day and night do these images suggest?

5. Does night or day seem to triumph in this speech? What does this tell us about what Macbeth is thinking at this point in the play?

Imagery	Meaning	Interpretation	Effect on the audience
'We have scorched the snake, not killed it' (line 13)	The snake has been cut, but not killed.	The threat is potentially still dangerous – and is also now angry at being injured.	The audience may feel the danger and fear of reprisal that lie ahead for the Macbeths.
'Better be with the dead … / Than on the torture of the mind to lie / In restless ecstasy.' (lines 19–22)			
'ere the bat hath flown / His cloistered flight' (lines 40–41)			
'ere to black Hecate's summons / The shard-born beetle with his drowsy hums / Hath rung night's yawning peal' (lines 41–43)			

PUTTING DETAILS TO USE

Haunted by guilt – the ghost at the banquet

Throughout Act 3, Macbeth is a haunted man. He is haunted both by the guilt of having ordered the murder of his friend, Banquo, and by the ghost of Banquo himself. Scene 4 is one of the most famous in the play.

1 Read Scene 4 and note down as many words as you can think of to describe Macbeth's reaction when he sees the ghost.

2 In line 50, Macbeth says: '**Thou can'st not say I did it**'. Who do you think Macbeth is addressing this line to? Why do you think this?

   a   the ghost
   b   the guests
   c   Lady Macbeth
   d   himself
   e   the servants.

3 a   How does Lady Macbeth respond to Macbeth's behaviour (lines 58–73)?
   b   How does she explain his behaviour to the guests?
   c   Why do you think she makes these excuses for his behaviour?

4 When Ross asks Macbeth '**What sights, my lord?**', Lady Macbeth reacts by saying '**I pray you speak not**' (line 117). Why do you think she says this?

5 Do you think the ghost is real or just in Macbeth's imagination?

   a   Find evidence from Act 3 Scene 4 to suggest whether the ghost is real or a product of Macbeth's imagination.
   b   Draw a 'ghost' in the middle of a blank sheet, and inside it write the question 'Banquo's ghost: real or imagined?' Create a mind map by writing your evidence in the space around it. Use quotations from the play as well as your own words.
   c   What does the evidence suggest?

The Macbeths – a turning point?

At the end of Scene 4. Lady Macbeth tells the guests to leave and she and Macbeth are left alone. This will be the last time we see the couple together.

1 On a copy of the text, highlight and annotate key words and phrases that indicate what is in Macbeth's mind. What does he seem determined to do?

2 Write a list of your own words to describe Macbeth's thoughts and feelings at the end of this scene.

 Watch a video exploring the end of Scene 4 on Cambridge Elevate.

Thou can'st not say I did it; never shake Thy gory locks at me!

Macbeth: Act 3 Scene 4, lines 50–51

Learning checkpoint

The relationship between Macbeth and his wife seems to change at this point in the play. Write a paragraph answering the question:

How has the relationship between Macbeth and Lady Macbeth changed between Act 1 and Act 3?

Think about these questions before you write:

a Who seems to be in control at the end of this scene? Find evidence in the text to support your ideas.

b How does the language in this short episode suggest the relationship between Macbeth and Lady Macbeth has changed? Find evidence in the text to support your ideas.

The influence of the supernatural

1 The following table lists the events in the first three acts of *Macbeth* that could be seen as supernatural. Copy and complete the table with examples of each supernatural event. Add any other types of event that you can think of and give examples.

Supernatural event	Occurrence in play
Witches	Act 1 Scene 1: the Witches agree to meet Macbeth
ghostly appearances	
dreams/nightmares	
prophecies	
visions	
noises	
unexpected weather	
strange events	

I pray you, speak not; he grows worse and worse.

Lady Macbeth: Act 3 Scene 4, line 117

2 Work in pairs or small groups. Find a short extract from Act 3 that includes references to unnatural events, the supernatural, witchcraft or evil. On a copy of the extract, annotate the text to show how Shakespeare fills the verse with imagery of evil and darkness.

3 Now take your analysis of the text one step further.

a Perform some of the lines. Experiment with ways of speaking that emphasise the 'unnatural' elements. Remember – you are trying to grab the audience's attention.

b Do you think that these lines were intended to scare the audience, or do they have a different purpose?

4 Look back over the first three acts. How important do you think the Witches are in *Macbeth*? Write a paragraph offering an explanation and interpretation. Think about the following questions:

a How and when do the Witches influence Macbeth? What do they say and do?

b How do the supernatural scenes and **themes** create a particular mood or tone in the play? What do they add to the experience for an audience.

Why does Hecate appear?

Macbeth and his wife commit many of their evil deeds in Act 3, this time without the Witches playing a part. The Witches' sudden appearance in Scene 5 is rather surprising. In this scene, Hecate, goddess of witchcraft, rebukes the three Witches for their '**trade and traffic with Macbeth**' without her knowledge or permission.

1 Look at these extracts from Hecate's speech in Scene 5.

And which is worse, all you have done
Hath been but for a wayward son,
Spiteful and wrathful, who, as others do,
Loves for his own ends, not for you.

Hecate: Act 3 Scene 5, lines 10–14

He shall spurn fate, scorn death, and bear
His hopes 'bove wisdom, grace and fear.
And you all know, security
Is mortals' chiefest enemy.

Hecate: Act 3 Scene 5, lines 30–34

What do these words tell you about Macbeth?

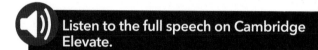
Listen to the full speech on Cambridge Elevate.

2 What does Hecate's speech tell the audience about what is going to happen to Macbeth? What effect does that have?

3 a In what way is this scene a dramatic moment in the play?

b How does the scene add to or detract from the action of the play?

4 Many productions of *Macbeth* leave out this scene or cut lines from it. If you were directing a production of the play, would you:

a keep it in

b cut it down

c leave it out?

Give reasons for your decision.

Read more about the themes and ideas in *Macbeth* in Unit 9.

Connect to the text

Act 3 Scene 5 is Hecate's only appearance in the play and the whole scene is rather unexpected. Some experts think that in fact this scene was added later by a different writer, Thomas Middleton. Middleton lived at the same time as Shakespeare, and the two men may have worked together on other plays. At the time, it was quite common for more than one person to contribute to the writing of a play.

Contexts

In Shakespeare's time, it was widely believed that witches could cast spells that might kill farm animals or cause crops to fail. Experts think that some old people were accused of witchcraft by their neighbours because they depended on the help and generosity of those neighbours, which could be a burden.

Plays about the supernatural were very popular in Shakespeare's times. Many people would have been convinced that they had, at one time or another, been cursed by witches. In 1590, it was discovered that a group of accused witches were planning to kill King James I. This led James to write *Daemonologie*, a book on witchcraft, and there was a dramatic rise in the numbers of people accused of being witches. In 1604, an Act of Parliament was passed making witchcraft punishable by death. It was against this background that Shakespeare wrote *Macbeth* – perhaps to please the king.

GETTING IT INTO WRITING

Writing about the supernatural

The supernatural is a key theme in the play, and one that you should be able to comment on in your writing. You will need to show that you understand how the supernatural is presented through the language that the **characters** use.

Look at this question:

To what extent are the Witches to blame for the evil actions of Macbeth and Lady Macbeth? How do the events of Act 3 affect our view of this question?

 Read the three sample paragraphs in response to this question.

a Which student has given the most developed and well explained answer?

b Identify the strengths of each response and the places where each one could be improved.

Student A

Macbeth is responsible for his own actions. Although the Witches tell of his future fortune as king, it was he who acted on this and 'played'st most foully for't'. The Witches tell him what the future holds, but Macbeth continues to commit the evil deeds that make the prophecies come true.

Student B

Meeting the Witches very obviously changes Macbeth. He is presented as a 'worthy' man until he meets the Witches. After meeting them and hearing their prophecies, he abandons his principles, kills the king and his friend, Banquo, whose children may threaten his reign.

Student C

Shakespeare uses the Witches to reveal Macbeth's tragic flaw – his ambition. When they 'hail' his future kingship, at first he is indecisive, but he works with determination and acts 'foully for't'. The Witches work as a dramatic device to further Macbeth's ambition, but their unclear prophecy (an example of equivocation) means that he and his own ambition are to blame for his actions.

 Drawing together the ideas that you have explored in this unit, write your own extended answer to the same question. Practise doing this in about 45 minutes.

✔ Learning checkpoint

How will I know I've done this well?

✔ **The best answers** will explore how Shakespeare shapes our interpretation of Macbeth and his wife. They will take evidence from different parts of the text and comment on how the Witches influence the Macbeths and our view of their actions.

✔ **Good answers** will show a clear understanding of how Shakespeare uses the Witches to influence events and characters. They will use well-chosen examples from a number of scenes in the play.

✔ **Weaker answers** will only comment on the events in the play without using many examples or mentioning why Shakespeare might use them to affect the audience. They might offer an opinion, but will not justify that viewpoint with examples.

✔ Complete this assignment on Cambridge Elevate.

Thou hast it now, King, Cawdor, Glamis, all,
As the weïrd women promised, and I fear
Thou played'st most foully for't

Banquo: Act 3 Scene 1, lines 1–3

GETTING FURTHER

A tyrant takes control

1 Macbeth's coronation is not shown on stage, but we know that it takes place at Scone between Acts 2 and 3. Imagine you are a Scottish nobleman who attended the coronation. Write an account describing:

a   the events and mood of the day
b   your thoughts and feelings about the coronation and Macbeth
c   what you intend to do now that he is king.

2 Macbeth wants to keep the murder of Banquo **'from the common eye'** (Act 3 Scene 1, line 124). In pairs, discuss what the **'sundry weighty reasons'** (line 125) might be that prevent him from carrying out the murder himself.

> **Key terms**
>
> **irony:** directly contradicting the truth (on purpose or by accident).

3 Act 3 Scene 6 is an account of the tyranny that the people of Scotland are now experiencing under Macbeth's rule. Lennox and the Lord speak with **irony** and hint at Macbeth's involvement in what has happened.

a   In small groups, read the conversation between Lennox and the Lord. Use gestures and facial expressions to show what the two men really mean.
b   Speaking out against a tyrant is risky. Compare Lennox's behaviour and words here with his behaviour in Act 3 Scene 4. What has changed?

4 When Macbeth first hears the news that Duncan has made him Thane of Cawdor, he says:

If chance will have me king, why chance may crown me
Without my stir.

Macbeth: Act 1 Scene 3, lines 142–143

What do you think Macbeth means? What is the 'chance' he is referring to?

Masking the business from the common eye
For sundry weighty reasons.

5 Consider what might have happened if Macbeth had not acted on the Witches' prophecies and '**played'st most foully for't**'.

Copy and complete the table below to organise your ideas.

Off-stage action

The word 'obscene' comes from the Latin meaning 'off stage'. Murders, battles and sexual activity took place off stage in the ancient Greek and Roman theatre. The modern English use of the word describes things that offend accepted standards of decency, including political issues such as unemployment and poverty.

1 Why do you think Shakespeare includes scenes that **report** events rather than showing them on stage? Consider the following:

a   dramatic reasons, such as theatrical staging in Shakespeare's times
b   political reasons.

2 Write a list of events that take place off stage in the first three acts of Macbeth.

Prophecy	Reference	Brought about 'most foully'?	Would/could it have happened anyway? How?
Macbeth becomes Thane of Cawdor.	Act 1 Scene 3, line 103	No	Yes – Duncan decided to promote Macbeth due to the betrayal of the previous thane.
Macbeth becomes King of Scotland.	Act 2, Scene 4, line 31	Yes – Macbeth killed Duncan and Lady Macbeth framed the king's guards for the murder.	Yes – Macbeth seems to have been in the line of succession. Also, Scottish kings were elected ('named') by the thanes, so he might have been chosen anyway after Duncan's death.
Banquo shall not be king, but his heirs shall be kings.			

4

Act 4: Resistance and revenge

How does Shakespeare plot Macbeth's downfall?

Your progress in this unit:
- identify the ways that Shakespeare contrasts Macbeth and Lady Macbeth with other characters
- explore the dramatic contrasts in Act 4
- explore how Shakespeare uses imagery of chaos and turmoil
- develop your skills in writing appropriate written responses.

GETTING STARTED – THE PLAY AND YOU

Looking into the future

Do you know what star sign you were born under? Do you ever look at your horoscope to find out what is going to happen in your life?

1 Work in groups or as a whole class. Discuss the following questions:

a Why do some people look at their horoscopes? Why might they want to know what is going to happen in the future?

b Do you believe that your future is already planned out for you, by 'fate' or some higher power? Or do you think you have control over what happens to you?

c Is it a good thing or a bad thing to know what is going to happen to you in the future? Why?

GETTING CLOSER – FOCUSING ON DETAILS

Dramatic contrasts

Act 4 has just three scenes, but is full of dramatic contrasts – from the conjuring up of spirits by the Witches to violent murder, from a personal test of character and loyalty to deepest grief. Macbeth appears in only one scene, but everything that happens in this act seems to tell us something about him.

Read the following summary of what happens in Act 4, and then read Act 4.

Scene 1

Macbeth confronts the Witches and demands they answer his questions. They tell him to fear Macduff, but that nobody '**born of woman**' can harm him; he will remain king until Birnam Wood comes to Dunsinane (where his castle is). But Macbeth is appalled when he is shown a vision of Banquo's descendants as kings. Macbeth discovers that Macduff has fled Scotland. He orders the killing of Macduff's whole family.

Scene 2

Ross visits Lady Macduff. After he leaves, Lady Macduff and her children are murdered by Macbeth's men.

Scene 3

In exile in England, Malcolm is at first suspicious of Macduff, but after testing him he is convinced of Macduff's loyalty. He pledges to be a good king and says that the English will send an army to defeat Macbeth. Ross arrives and informs Macduff of the murder of his wife and children. Malcolm is appalled at Macbeth's cruelty. Overcome with grief, Macduff vows to kill Macbeth himself.

1 At the end of Act 3, Macbeth announces his intention of consulting with the Witches again. In the first scene of Act 4, we see him confronting them:

I conjure you by that which you profess,
Howe'er you come to know it, answer me.
Though you untie the winds and let them fight
Against the churches, though the yeasty waves
Confound and swallow navigation up,
Though bladed corn be lodged and trees blown
    down,
Though castles topple on their warders' heads,
Though palaces and pyramids do slope
Their heads to their foundations, though the
    treasure
Of nature's germen tumble altogether
Even till destruction sicken: answer me
To what I ask you.

Macbeth: Act 4 Scene 1, lines 49–60

a   Why do you think Macbeth visits the Witches again at this point in the play?
b   Macbeth twice asks the Witches to '**answer me**'. What does he so badly want to know?

2 a   List the images that Shakespeare creates in this speech.
b   Identify and note down the key words that help create these images.
c   What is the **overall** idea or image created by this speech?

3 Read the speech out loud.

a   What is the effect of the repetition of the word 'though'?
b   What features of the language make it sound like a spell or incantation?

4 What does this speech suggest about Macbeth's state of mind when he comes to visit the Witches?

'Seek to know no more'

Macbeth is obsessed by one thing: the desire to know what is going to happen in the future. He demands that the Witches tell him what he wants to know. The Witches conjure up spirits to reveal the answers that Macbeth seeks.

1 Copy and complete the following table to explain what Macbeth is told by each of the spirits and how he reacts to each prophecy. Include key words and short quotations to support your answers.

What does Macbeth find out?	How does he react?	Key words/ quotations
The first spirit tells him that …		
The second spirit tells him that …		
The third spirit tells him that …		

No boasting like a fool;
This deed I'll do before the purpose cool

Macbeth: Act 4 Scene 1, lines 152–153

2 After showing him the three spirits, the Witches tell Macbeth that he should '**Seek to know no more**' (line 102).

   a Despite their warning, Macbeth says that his heart '**Throbs to know one thing**'. What is it that he wants to know?

   b The Witches show him a vision to answer his question. Describe in your own words what Macbeth sees in this 'show'.

   c What answer does the vision give to his question?

   d Identify key words in lines 111–123 that reveal his reaction to what he has seen.

Deadly decisions

1 At the end of Act 4 Scene 1, a messenger arrives to tell Macbeth that Macduff has fled to England. Macbeth has already determined to kill Macduff (lines 81–85). What does he decide to do now?

2 Read the following extract from Macbeth's soliloquy at the end of Scene 1. Shakespeare seems to be expressing the same idea in four different ways. Summarise in your own words what Macbeth is saying in this speech.

> The flighty purpose never is o'ertook
> Unless the deed go with it. From this moment,
> The very firstlings of my heart shall be
> The firstlings of my hand. And even now
> To crown my thoughts with acts, be it thought
>   and done …
>   No boasting like a fool;
> This deed I'll do before the purpose cool

Macbeth: Act 4 Scene 1, lines 144–153

3 Write some notes to summarise how Macbeth's character has changed by this point in Act 4. In what ways are his thoughts and behaviour different from earlier in the play? Find evidence from Act 4 Scene 1 to support your comments. Include short quotes.

Contexts

> And yet the eighth appears, who bears a glass
> Which shows me many more. And some I see,
> That two-fold balls and treble sceptres carry.

Macbeth: Act 4 Scene 1, lines 118–120

In Shakespeare's day, historians thought that James I was descended from Banquo. James was king of Scotland and England ('**two-fold balls**' – the orbs of the crown jewels) and ruled over three kingdoms – Scotland, England and Ireland ('**treble sceptres**'). The eight kings that the Witches show Macbeth represent James's ancestors and the '**glass**' (mirror) carried by the eighth king shows the future of the Stuart dynasty – the royal house to which James belonged.

You may find it helpful to record your notes in a table like this, to refer to when you are revising or writing about Macbeth's character and **characterisation**.

How has Macbeth changed by the end of his meeting with the Witches in Act 4?	Evidence from the text

PUTTING DETAILS TO USE

Ross – good or bad?

Shakespeare's **characters** are open to interpretation because the text of the plays does not provide **stage directions** to explain their thoughts and intentions. This allows the director and actors to decide for themselves what motivates a character.

Act 4 Scene 2 begins with Ross breaking the news to Lady Macduff that her husband has fled to England. In Scene 3, he brings the news of her murder to Macduff. Some productions present Ross as a good character and some portray him as one of Macbeth's spies.

1 Draw a simple outline figure on a large sheet of paper. Use this to write brief notes for an actor playing Ross in Act 4 Scene 2.

a   In the head area, write what Ross is **thinking** as he visits Lady Macduff and her children.

b   In the chest area, write what he is **feeling**.

c   In his arm and leg area, write what you think he is **doing** (his actions and gestures).

Develop your notes by adding quotations from the scene to support your ideas and instructions.

2 Now draw another blank figure. Follow the same process as in Question 1, but this time outline how your actor should present Ross in the opposite way.

Connect to the text

Roman Polanski's 1971 film of the play showed Ross working with Macbeth, betraying the Macduffs. He leaves Lady Macduff in tears, but he is just pretending. He is then shown signalling to the murderers to go in the castle and kill the family. This shows how Macbeth's evil influence and control spreads throughout Scotland. This is, of course, only one interpretation. Some people have argued that making Ross an evil character is wrong because later in the play his actions suggest he is genuinely upset by the horrific actions of Macbeth and his followers. How do you interpret the character of Ross – good or bad?

Stands Scotland where it did?

Macduff: Act 4 Scene 3, line 165

Scene 3 – delivering bad news

In Act 4 Scene 3, Shakespeare once again uses the words and actions of different characters to give his audience information about how Macbeth's own character is developing. Ross visits Malcolm in England. Macduff has also gone there to support Malcolm's claim to the Scottish throne. Once again, Ross acts as the messenger.

1 Look at Ross's answer to Macduff's question: **'Stands Scotland where it did?'** (lines 166–175).

   a Draw up a table with two columns, headed 'Positive' and 'Negative'. In the table, list the key words that Ross uses as he describes the state of Scotland. Put the words in the columns according to whether they have positive (e.g. 'mother') or negative (e.g. 'grave') **connotations**.

   b What do these key words suggest about what Scotland should be (but isn't) and what Scotland shouldn't be (but is).

2 Ross delays telling Macduff about the murder of his wife and children by saying that they are **'well'** and **'at peace'**.

   a In pairs, discuss why he might not tell Macduff the news immediately.

   b What does this delay add to the scene (consider the **dramatic irony** and how it might make the audience feel).

3 Eventually, Ross blurts out the truth:

> Your castle is surprised; your wife and babes
> Savagely slaughtered. To relate the manner
> Were on the quarry of these murdered deer
> To add the death of you.

Ross: Act 4 Scene 3, lines 206–209

How does his language here contrast with his earlier speeches?

Key terms

stage directions: text in the script of a play that helps the director and actors realise in performance what the writer wanted to happen on stage to convey a particular interpretation.

> Your castle is surprised;
> your wife and babes
> Savagely slaughtered.

Ross: Act 4 Scene 3, lines 206–207

The longest scene

Act 4 Scene 3 is the longest scene in the play (243 lines). It is structured as a series of conversations.

1 Look at this list of events from Act 4 Scene 3. They are not in the correct order.

a Malcolm declares his own true character and is ready to invade Scotland.

b Ross reports the murder of Macduff's family.

c Malcolm claims that his own character is worse than Macbeth's.

d Ross reports the suffering of Scotland under Macbeth's rule.

e Malcolm expresses his suspicions about Macduff's loyalty.

f Macduff vows revenge and Malcolm declares that the time has come to overthrow Macbeth.

g In an outburst of anger, Macduff says that Malcolm is not fit to rule Scotland.

h Malcolm and a doctor talk about the saintliness of the English King, Edward, and of his power to heal people.

On a copy of the following table, put the sections of the scene **a** to **h** in the correct order. Add the approximate line numbers for each section. Give brief details of what happens in each section.

Section	Lines	What happens
1e Malcolm expresses his suspicions about Macduff's loyalty.	1–37	Malcolm draws attention to the closeness of Macbeth and Macduff in the past and suggests that Macduff may be a traitor too.
2		

How is Malcolm's character presented?

Malcolm is Duncan's eldest son. Although the sons of kings did not have an automatic right to inherit the throne in ancient Scotland, it was still common for a son to succeed his father. Duncan had named Malcolm as his heir, but Macbeth has won the throne instead.

Malcolm is sometimes portrayed as a saviour - almost Christ-like - who returns to Scotland to defeat the devil, in the form of Macbeth. The following images contribute to this idea:

> new sorrows
> Strike heaven on the face …

Macduff: Act 4 Scene 3, lines 5–6

> To offer up a weak, poor, innocent lamb
> T'appease an angry god.

Malcolm: Act 4 Scene 3, lines 16–17

> Angels are bright still, though the brightest fell.

Malcolm: Act 4 Scene 3, line 22

> Though all things foul would wear
> the brows of grace

Malcolm: Act 4 Scene 3, line 23

1 Read the rest of the scene and identify other references to the devil or to a saviour figure.

2 How does this help to suggest a struggle between good and evil?

 **Read more on characters and characterisation in *Macbeth* in Unit 8.**

Is Macduff sincere?

At first, Malcolm is suspicious of Macduff. After all, Macduff has previously been a faithful friend to Macbeth – the man that Malcolm believes killed his father and stole his throne.

1 Read Act 4 Scene 3, lines 8–31. Copy and complete the following table to demonstrate how Malcolm's words imply his suspicion of Macduff's loyalty.

What Malcolm says	How it implies suspicion of Macduff
'This tyrant, whose sole name blisters our tongues, / Was one thought honest; you have loved him well'	Although Macduff appears to be honest, Macbeth did too and turned out not to be. Macduff was a friend of Macbeth, which may mean that he still is and this is a trap.
'He hath not touched you yet'	
'A good and virtuous nature may recoil / In an imperial charge'	
'Though all things foul would wear the brows of grace'	
'Why in that rawness left you wife and child'	
'Let not my jealousies be your dishonours, / But mine own safeties'	

Let not my jealousies be
your dishonours,
But mine own safeties

Malcolm: Act 4 Scene 3, lines 29–30

2 Read Act 4 Scene 3, lines 44–114.

    a How does Malcolm test Macduff's loyalty?

    b How does Macduff respond to what Malcolm tells him? How does the language of lines 102–114 suggest how Macduff feels about what Malcolm has said?

3 Read Act 4 Scene 3, lines 114–137.

    a How does Malcolm reply to Macduff's condemnation?

    b How and why does Malcolm's opinion of Macduff change because of Macduff's reaction?

From Scotland to England

Act 4 Scene 3 is the only scene in the play that takes place outside Scotland. The conversation between Malcolm and Macduff at the beginning of the scene is rich in Christian **imagery**, which contrasts England with the images of chaos and turmoil in Scotland.

1 Write two headings – 'England' and 'Scotland' – in the middle of a blank sheet of paper, with enough space around them to write. Around each heading, write examples of words or images used in this scene to describe England and Scotland.

2 Work in small groups. Discuss how Shakespeare uses language in this scene to suggest the difference between the English court and Macbeth's court in Scotland.

 Read more about language in *Macbeth* in Unit 10.

GETTING IT INTO WRITING

Contrasting the Macbeths and the Macduffs

The scene in Macduff's castle (Act 4 Scene 2) shows a happy family. It has been suggested that Shakespeare uses this scene to contrast with the lives and characters of Macbeth and Lady Macbeth.

Look at the following question and at the three responses.

How does Shakespeare contrast the characters of Macbeth and Macduff?

Response 1

Macbeth's orders in Act 4 Scene 2 lead to the horrific death of Macduff's family. Like historical tyrants, Macbeth is seen punishing innocents. The audience will feel sorry for the victims and come to despise Macbeth even more.

Response 2

Shakespeare uses the Macduff family to contrast with the Macbeths. Although Lady Macduff is concerned that her family is 'fatherless' due to Macduff's absence, the relationship between her and her son is strong. The family suggests that Macduff is caring. Macbeth's actions suggest that he is not.

Response 3

Shakespeare decides to show the violence against Macduff's family on stage. Most of the other violence in the play occurs off stage and is reported. When the son says: 'He has killed me, mother.' Shakespeare uses the human suffering to make the evil actions of Macbeth realistic and effective for the audience.

Whither should I fly?
I have done no harm.

Lady Macduff:
Act 4 Scene 2, lines 70–71

1 Which of the three responses do you think is the best? Why?

2 Using a copy of the following table, identify the strengths and weaknesses of each response. Suggest how each response could be improved.

Response	Strengths	Weaknesses	Suggestions for improvement
1			
2			
3			

3 Drawing together the ideas that you have explored in this unit, write your own extended answer to one of the following questions. Practise writing your response in no more than 45 minutes.

In Act 4 Scene 2, how does Shakespeare use the Macduff family as a contrast to Macbeth and to draw attention to the kind of king he is?

Looking back over Act 4, how do the various contrasts encourage the audience to think about kingship?

You will want to consider:

a Malcolm and Banquo
b information about the English king, Edward the Confessor (even though he never appears on stage)
c what Macduff says about Duncan
d the fact that Malcolm is Duncan's son.

 Complete this assignment on Cambridge Elevate.

 Learning checkpoint

How will I know I've done this well?

✔ **The best answers** will explore what Shakespeare does to make contrasts with Macbeth. They will look at specific scenes and comment on how details of tyrannical actions (both on stage and off stage) and language are included throughout the play to affect the audience.

✔ **Good answers** will show a clear understanding of what Shakespeare does to show contrasts with Macbeth to the audience using well-chosen examples from a number of scenes in the play.

✔ **Weaker answers** will only comment on the contrasts to Macbeth in the play without using many examples or mentioning why Shakespeare might use them to affect the audience.

GETTING FURTHER

Macduff's family

Unlike Banquo's family, we actually see Macduff's wife and children at home in their castle, in Act 4 Scene 2.

1 Write a paragraph or two to explain why Shakespeare might have chosen to show this aspect of Macduff's life.

2 Imagine you are directing the play. How would you stage this scene? What effect do you want it to have on the audience?

    a Make some brief director's notes under various headings (e.g. 'Set', 'Lighting', 'Sound', 'Movement', 'Voice')

    b Explain why you have made each of these decisions. Use evidence from the play to support your choices.

A good king versus a bad king

Look closely at Act 4 Scene 3, lines 57–60, in which Malcolm lists the evils of Macbeth:

- **'bloody'** (murderous)
- **'luxurious'** (lecherous)
- **'avaricious'** (greedy)
- **'false'**
- **'deceitful'**
- **'sudden'** (violent)
- **'malicious'**
- **'every sin / That has a name'** (a reference to the Seven Deadly Sins: wrath, greed, sloth, pride, lust, envy and gluttony)

1 What is the effect of listing all these 'evils' in this way? How does it shape the audience's opinion of Macbeth?

Luxurious, avaricious, false, deceitful, Sudden, malicious

Malcolm: Act 4 Scene 3, lines 58–59

Malcolm refers to Macbeth as '**black**' (line 52) and '**devilish**' (line 117). By contrast, he says the English king is '**full of grace**' (line 161). Shakespeare's audience would have known that Edward the Confessor was once the patron saint of England, and that his tomb in Westminster Abbey had been a place of pilgrimage.

2 Find references to King Edward in Act 4 Scene 3 and write a paragraph describing how Shakespeare sets up a **juxtaposition** between Edward and Macbeth.

3 At the beginning of the play, we hear of Macbeth's qualities before we see him. Here, we do not see King Edward - we only learn about him through the words of others. Why do you think Shakespeare does not bring Edward on stage?

4 Malcolm lists the qualities of a good king:

> The king-becoming graces –
> As justice, verity, temp'rance, stableness,
> Bounty, perseverance, mercy, lowliness,
> Devotion, patience, courage, fortitude –

Malcolm: Act 4 Scene 3, lines 91–94

a What does this list tell us about Shakespeare's ideas of kingship and those of his society?
b How might a modern audience respond differently to this list of virtues from the audience that saw the first performance of the play?

c How does this list of virtues contrast with the list of Macbeth's vices? What is the effect of this juxtaposition?

5 Write a short paragraph of no more than 100 words to explain how Shakespeare uses lists, contrasts and juxtaposition in this scene. Include the effect they have.

6 Shakespeare includes a reference to the power that English monarchs were thought to have to heal the sick (Act 4 Scene 3, lines 141–145). Many people believed that the monarch was chosen by God and that the power to heal was evidence of this. Malcolm says:

> To the succeeding royalty he leaves
> The healing benediction.

Malcolm: Act 4 Scene 3, lines 157–158

a Work in pairs. Discuss why Shakespeare might have included this reference to healing in the play.
b What might Shakespeare have been saying to his audience about their king, James I?

Key terms

juxtaposition: the placement of two ideas or things near each other to invite comparison or contrast.

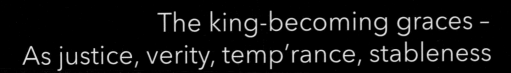

The king-becoming graces –
As justice, verity, temp'rance, stableness

5

Act 5: Endings and beginnings

How does the play end?

- understand the factors that lead to Macbeth's downfall
- consider how Lady Macbeth's character has changed
- explore the moral context and messages of the play
- analyse the use of dark and violent imagery and language
- develop written response skills.

GETTING STARTED – THE PLAY AND YOU

Sympathy or judgement?

Every day the news reports cases of people doing something wrong or committing serious crimes. In most cases you may not think there is any reason to feel sorry for those people. You will probably feel that they deserve their punishment. But are there any exceptions to this?

1 Work in small groups. Discuss the following questions.

   a Think of examples in the recent news where you may have felt sympathy for someone who has committed a terrible crime. Why did you feel that way?

   b Under what circumstances might you feel sympathy for someone who had done something bad? How would you judge?

GETTING CLOSER – FOCUS ON DETAILS

Bringing it all together

Act 5 is packed with dramatic moments as the play reaches its climax and conclusion. Read the following summary of what happens in Act 5, and then read Act 5.

Scene 1
Lady Macbeth is very ill. Sleepwalking and talking in her sleep, she sees visions of blood on her hands. The Doctor and her Gentlewoman realise, through the things she says, that she is guilty of Duncan's murder, but they are unable to help with her troubled behaviour.

Scene 2
The English army has marched on Scotland. Macbeth has defended his castle at Dunsinane and is prepared for a siege, even though men are deserting him.

Scene 3
Macbeth is furious that Malcolm is approaching. He is told that Lady Macbeth cannot be cured.

Scene 4
Malcolm hears of many deserters from Macbeth's army. He orders his army to cut down the boughs of the trees from Birnam Wood and use them as camouflage when marching to Dunsinane.

Scene 5
Macbeth hears a scream and is informed that his wife has committed suicide. His reply is subtle; he has to concentrate on the coming fight. He is shaken by the next message he receives – Birnam Wood is coming to Dunsinane, just as the Witches predicted.

Scenes 6 and 7
The battle begins and Macbeth fights fearlessly, killing many just as he did in the battle before the play begins. Although Macbeth's army is losing, nobody seems able to kill Macbeth.

Scene 8
Finally, Macbeth meets Macduff face to face in battle. They fight and Macduff reveals that he is not '**of woman born**' – he was born by caesarean section. On hearing this, Macbeth's courage deserts him. He is killed by Macduff.

Scene 9
Macduff produces the head of Macbeth for Malcolm and hails him as the new king of Scotland. Malcolm invites all to attend his coronation.

What, will these hands ne'er be clean?

Lady Macbeth: Act 5 Scene 1, line 37

Talking about Macbeth

Just like in Act 1, Macbeth does not appear in Act 5 until the third scene. This delay gives the audience a chance to hear what the other **characters** say about him. The repetition of this dramatic device allows the audience to make a contrast.

1 a Create a table to list significant words and phrases used by other characters to describe or respond to Macbeth before his appearances in Acts 1 and 5.
   b Overall, how is Macbeth described in Act 1? How is he described in Act 5?
   c What effect does this contrast have on the way we see Macbeth?

Comments about/ responses to Macbeth in Act 1	Comments about/ responses to Macbeth in Act 5
'… brave Macbeth – well he deserves that name …' (Captain: Scene 2, line 16)	'the tyrant' (Menteith: Scene 2, line 11)

Lady Macbeth sleepwalks

Act 5 begins with one of the most famous scenes of any Shakespeare play. Watched by her Gentlewoman and a Doctor, Lady Macbeth sleepwalks, talking in her sleep about the '**deeds**' she has committed.

1 Look at these two statements by Lady Macbeth – one from Act 2 and one from Act 5:

A little water clears us of this deed. How easy is it then!

Lady Macbeth: Act 2 Scene 2, lines 70-71

What, will these hands ne'er be clean?

Lady Macbeth: Act 5 Scene 1, line 37

a In pairs, discuss how Shakespeare uses language to make a connection between these two points in the play.
b What does the contrast between these two quotations suggest about the change that has come over Lady Macbeth by the beginning of Act 5?

 Watch a video of Lady Macbeth's sleepwalking scene on Cambridge Elevate.

 Read more about language in *Macbeth* in Unit 10.

2 Read through what Lady Macbeth says in Act 5 Scene 1, and make a note of any references she makes to earlier incidents in the play. Use a table like this.

Reference	Event referred to
'Fie, my lord, fie, a soldier and afeard?'	Macbeth was scared at the thought of killing Duncan

a   What does your completed table suggest about Lady Macbeth's state of mind? What is troubling her?

b   What evidence is there to support your idea?

3 Look at these lines from Act 2:

> These deeds must not be thought
> After these ways; so, it will make us mad.

Lady Macbeth: Act 2 Scene 2, lines 37–38

How do the events of Act 5 Scene 1 make you reconsider the significance of lines such as this?

The Doctor and the Gentlewoman

The sleepwalking scene begins with a Doctor and a Gentlewoman speaking to each other. This is one of the few passages in Macbeth where Shakespeare uses **prose** rather than **verse**.

1 Why do you think Shakespeare uses prose in this scene? Look at the possible reasons in the table below.

a   Rank them in order 1 to 4, with the most convincing as number 1.

b   Find evidence from the text to support your decisions.

c   Add an idea of your own. Try to justify it with evidence from the text.

Key terms

prose: writing that follows the style of normal speech.

verse: writing that has a particular rhyme, pattern or rhythm.

Rank	Reason	Evidence
	Shakespeare is showing an informal conversation; this is gossip rather than the language of the court.	
	Shakespeare wants to make this scene seem more 'real' for the audience. They speak in prose, so that the audience is drawn into what they are saying and sympathises with Lady Macbeth.	
	The Doctor and the Gentlewoman are servants and Shakespeare wants to show this.	
	Shakespeare wants to demonstrate that the normal rules have broken down and that formality and etiquette has given way to disorder and rumour.	
	I think the characters speak in prose in this scene because …	

2 Later in the scene, the Doctor and the Gentlewoman both start speaking in **blank verse**.

  a Identify the point where their speech changes.
  b Why do you think Shakespeare introduced this change here?

3 Shakespeare sometimes uses prose for dramatic effect or when presenting particular types of characters. How does the choice of prose affect the mood of this scene?

 Watch an interview with the Gentlewoman on Cambridge Elevate.

 Connect to the text

Shakespeare mostly writes his plays in verse (rather like dramatic poetry). However, he does sometimes use prose to create special effects. Prose is often used to present certain types of characters:

- those of lower status (such as servants)
- those who are seen as 'mad'
- entertainers ('clowns' or 'fools') whose job is to make the audience laugh, such as the Porter in Act 2 of *Macbeth*.

Sometimes prose is used to establish a contrast between the poetry spoken in some scenes by characters of higher status and scenes that are less formal and more 'realistic'.

PUTTING DETAILS TO USE

Macbeth reflects on life

Macbeth retreats to his castle. A sequence of messengers deliver bad news about the approaching English army and Macbeth begins to doubt the Witches' prophecies.

His outward mood changes from weariness and doubt to threat and bravado, but he is determined to fight on, whatever may happen. Through a series of **soliloquies** Shakespeare allows us to hear his private thoughts:

> I have lived long enough. My way of life
> Is fall'n into the sere, the yellow leaf,
> And that which should accompany old age,
> As honour, love, obedience, troops of friends,
> I must not look to have; but in their stead,
> Curses, not loud but deep, mouth-honour, breath
> Which the poor heart would fain deny,
>   and dare not.

Macbeth: Act 5 Scene 3, lines 22-28

1 In this speech, Macbeth lists four things that people hope for in old age. What are they? Write a sentence about each one to explain what it would mean for an older person.

2 What does Macbeth expect instead of these things? How do these contrast with what other people hope for?

I have lived long enough. My way of life Is fall'n into the sere, the yellow leaf

Macbeth: Act 5 Scene 3, lines 22-23

3 What does the language of this speech suggest about Macbeth's outlook on life by this point in the play?

'Out, out, brief candle'

At the beginning of Scene 5, Macbeth hears women crying. However, he does not react to this:

I had almost forgot the taste of fears;
The time has been, my senses would have cooled
To hear a night-shriek and my fell of hair
Would at a dismal treatise rouse and stir
As life were in't. I have supped full with horrors;
Direness familiar to my slaughterous thoughts
Cannot once start me.

Macbeth: Act 5 Scene 5, lines 9–15

1 **a** What is the meaning of Macbeth's words in this speech?
   b Try rewriting these lines in your own words.
   c What does this speech tell us about how Macbeth's character has changed from earlier in the play?

When Seyton informs us that '**The queen, my lord, is dead**', Macbeth responds:

She should have died hereafter
There would have been a time for such a word.

Macbeth: Act 5 Scene 5, lines 16–17

In this **context**, the word 'should' could mean:

- she **ought** to have died later
- she **would have** died later **anyway**.

2 What do you think Macbeth might mean in each case?

3 What do these interpretations tell us about:

   a Macbeth's state of mind
   b Macbeth's relationship with Lady Macbeth?

4 Macbeth comments on the death of his wife in a short speech that reflects on the meaning of life (Act 5 Scene 5, lines 16–27).

   a What do you think Shakespeare is trying to convey to the audience through this speech?
   b The language here makes powerful use of **imagery**. Identify the images in the speech.
   c In a table like the following one, comment on what each image seems to be saying about human life.

Image	What does it say about life?

5 Macbeth compares human life to an actor on a stage (Act 5 Scene 5, lines 23–25). Why do you think Shakespeare chose to use this image at such an important moment of the play?

Watch a video of Macbeth's speech on Cambridge Elevate.

Key terms

blank verse: unrhymed verse with carefully placed stressed and unstressed syllables

Macbeth as 'tragic hero'

Many of Shakespeare's plays are called **tragedies**. A tragedy is built around the personality and career of a 'tragic hero'. The key points about a tragic hero can be summarised as follows:

- They are the central figure in the drama.
- It is their personality and decisions that make the events in the story happen.
- They usually have a secret flaw or weakness in their personality that causes a fatal mistake and leads to their downfall.
- They are at the centre of the action and they always die at the end of the play.

1 a Copy and complete the following table to show how the key elements of the 'tragic hero' can be seen in Macbeth.

b In what way does the weakness you have identified in Macbeth's character lead to his downfall?

A tragic hero ...	How does this apply to Macbeth?
is a man of power	As Thane of Glamis, Macbeth is a powerful and admired noble at the start of the play.
has a flaw or character weakness	
has a career that is impressive, frightening and finally sad	
becomes a tyrant and does terrible things	
has allies and enemies that are murdered, exiled or alienated	
becomes isolated and realises their flaw or mistake too late	
dies as a result of their own actions and character flaw	

I will not yield
To kiss the ground before
young Malcolm's feet

Macbeth: Act 5 Scene 9, lines 27–28

Look at the following points that three students have made about the character of Macbeth.

Student A

During the play, we see Macbeth apparently change from good to bad. In Act 1, the Captain describes him as 'brave' and Duncan calls him 'noble'. In Act 5, Malcolm calls him a 'butcher' and Macduff says he is a 'hell hound'.

Student B

The audience gets a special insight into the change in Macbeth as the play goes on. Through soliloquy we hear his private thoughts and therefore feel some sympathy for 'this dead butcher' (Act 5) who we see has a conscience and whose mind was 'full of scorpions' (Act 3).

Student C

The 'valiant', 'noble' and 'worthy' Macbeth we learn to admire in Act 1 becomes increasingly hard to empathise with. By Act 5 his 'sound and fury' has become too harsh and brutal for an audience to retain any sympathy for him and we are grateful when Macduff, who 'was from his mother's womb / Untimely ripped', cuts down 'the tyrant'.

2 Which response do you think is the most convincing and exploratory? Write a comment for each of them, identifying one strength and two things that could be improved.

In Scene 9, Macbeth realises that the end has come. The prophecies have falsely raised his hopes. Yet he remains defiant:

> I will not yield
> To kiss the ground before young Malcolm's feet
> And to be baited with the rabble's curse.
> Though Birnam Wood be come to Dunsinane
> And thou opposed being of no woman born,
> Yet I will try the last. Before my body,
> I throw my warlike shield.

Macbeth: Act 5 Scene 9, lines 27–33

3 How does the language in this – Macbeth's final speech – affect your view of him?

4 How do you think Shakespeare intended us to feel about Macbeth by the end of the play? Should we sympathise with him or not? Discuss this in small groups.

5 Make a list of anything that Macbeth says or does in Act 5 that seems admirable or that makes you sympathise with him. Give your reasons.

Learning checkpoint

Write one or two paragraphs explaining how Shakespeare shows changes in the characters of Macbeth and Lady Macbeth in Act 5.

How will I know I've done this well?

✔ You will have shown how Shakespeare uses language to convey information about character.

✔ You will have integrated at least one quotation to support each point you have made.

✔ You will have used examples from earlier in the play and made comparisons between aspects of character earlier in the play and in Act 5.

✔ You will have used key terminology and ensured accurate spelling and clear, well-punctuated sentences.

'The equivocation of the fiend'

Macbeth finally becomes aware that the Witches have misled him:

> I pull in resolution and begin
> To doubt th'equivocation of the fiend
> That lies like truth.

Macbeth: Act 5 Scene 5, lines 41–43

> And be these juggling fiends no more believed
> That palter with us in a double sense

Macbeth: Act 5 Scene 8, lines 19–20

1 Work in small groups. Discuss the following questions.

a What is Macbeth saying about what the Witches told him?

b Think about the Witches' prophecies, and about what happens in Scenes 5 and 8 of Act 5. In what way have the Witches lied **'like truth'**?

c Why might the Witches have intended to mislead Macbeth?

GETTING IT INTO WRITING

Lady Macbeth's obituary

An obituary is an account of someone's life that is published after their death. The purpose of an obituary is to:

- give factual details about a person's life
- summarise their achievements
- explore their personality, their strengths and weaknesses, in an objective way
- identify significant events and actions in their lives
- evaluate their contribution or the decisions they made in life
- suggest how, and for what, they will best be remembered.

2 Write an obituary of about 300 words for Lady Macbeth, to be published in the *Dunsinane Herald* the day after Malcolm's victory over Macbeth. Use some of the following starters to help you.

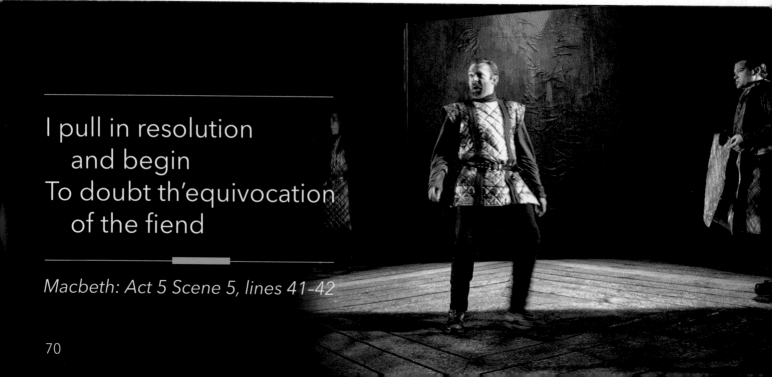

I pull in resolution
  and begin
To doubt th'equivocation
  of the fiend

Macbeth: Act 5 Scene 5, lines 41–42

Devil's Wife Dead at Dunsinane!

Lady Macbeth, who died along with her husband in yesterday's slaughter at Dunsinane, was born …

She first came to public attention when …

After she married Macbeth she …

When she first became queen she …

She has been described as …

Her Gentlewoman, who knew her well, has said that …

Some have said that she was …

Others have made excuses for her, such as …

The former queen died as a result of …

Her relationship with the late king was …

She will be remembered for …

Before you start writing, consider the following:

a What does Shakespeare's play actually tell us about Lady Macbeth?
b What information do we not know about her?
c What gaps will you have to fill in when writing your obituary?

 3 When articles and obituaries are published online, there is often an opportunity for people to leave comments underneath expressing their views. Add a couple of imaginary alternative views responding to your obituary.

 4 Drawing together the ideas that you have explored while studying Act 5, write an extended answer of no more than 300 words to **one** of the questions below. Practise writing your response in no more than 45 minutes.

> **In Act 5, how does Shakespeare show the development of Lady Macbeth's character?**
>
> **How does Act 5 contribute to the play's presentation of Macbeth as a tragic hero?**

✔ **Complete this assignment on Cambridge Elevate.**

✔ **Learning checkpoint**

How will I know I've done this well?

✔ **The best answers** will explore what Shakespeare does to show development in a character. They will look at specific scenes and comment on how details of character are conveyed through language, and the effect these have on the audience. They will use brief, well-chosen and integrated quotations to support the points being made.

✔ **Good answers** will show a clear understanding of what Shakespeare does to show different aspects of character to the audience using a range of examples and quotations from a number of scenes in the play.

✔ **Weaker answers** will only comment on the character's words and actions in the play without using many examples or quotations, or explaining how Shakespeare might use them to affect the audience.

GETTING FURTHER

The fall of a king

1 a What do you feel are the key factors that lead to Macbeth's downfall? Create a spider diagram to record your ideas.

 b Which factor(s) do you think are the most important? Give reasons for your choice.

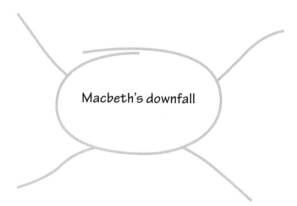

Macbeth's downfall

2 How far do you feel Macbeth is to blame for the terrible things that happen in the play? List reasons why he is to blame and why he is not. Weigh up the evidence, then write a response of no more than 300 words to answer the question.

 Watch a video about Macbeth's guilt on Cambridge Elevate.

3 Write a paragraph explaining how far you think the Witches are responsible for Macbeth's actions. Consider the following:

 a Are the Witches' prophecies genuine, or just vague statements?

 b Do the Witches really have any **supernatural** powers?

 c Why does Macbeth interpret the 'prophecies' in the way he does?

 d What choices does Macbeth have at various points in the play?

 Are the Witches to blame for Macbeth's actions? Watch a debate on Cambridge Elevate.

Thinking more about Lady Macbeth

1 Do you think Lady Macbeth's behaviour in Act 5 Scene 1 would come as a surprise to audiences? In what ways has Shakespeare prepared us for this development in her character? Find evidence from various scenes in the play to support your answer.

2 Look at the following grid, which contains a range of facts and opinions about the character of Lady Macbeth. Decide which of these are facts and which are opinions. Organise them into a two-column table.

Lay on, Macduff, And damned be him that first cries, 'Hold, enough!'

Macbeth: Act 5 Scene 8, lines 33–34

Lady Macbeth seems to show no pity towards humans or children.

Lady Macbeth behaves in an evil way.

When Lady Macbeth saw Duncan sleeping, he reminded her of her father.

Lady Macbeth claims she would rather kill her own child than break a promise.

She fears Macbeth is too kind to kill Duncan.

Without his wife, Macbeth would not have had the courage to murder Duncan.

Lady Macbeth pretends not to know Duncan is dead when his body is found in Act 2 Scene 3.

Lady Macbeth calls on evil spirits to assist her in Act 1 Scene 5.

Lady Macbeth criticises her husband for not correctly setting the guards up as Duncan's murderers.

Lady Macbeth pretends to faint in order to distract attention from Macbeth in Act 2 Scene 3.

Lady Macbeth drank alcohol before she drugged Duncan's bodyguards.

Lady Macbeth is stronger and more determined than Macbeth in Act 2.

3 Is Lady Macbeth a purely evil character, or is she worthy of some sympathy? Hold a class debate. Weigh the evidence carefully before reaching a conclusion.

Lady Macbeth in performance

Read these two different actors' thoughts on performing the role of Lady Macbeth:

I think first and foremost she's a wife, she's a homemaker, she's a very, very intelligent woman. I think that the audience have an affection for this woman to be able to see how far she and her husband fall. I think she's a very strong woman who's the backbone, the crutch of Macbeth. In their marriage she's been the backbone of him.

Alison McKenzie

She had no illusions about the evil she was embracing, but the thrill of it drew her back.

Judi Dench

1 Do you agree with these interpretations? Discuss this in pairs. Find evidence in the text to support your opinions.

2 Lady Macbeth is a challenging character to interpret and perform on stage. Directors and actors take very different views. Imagine you are directing a production of Macbeth. Prepare some brief notes for the actor playing Lady Macbeth. Include:

a   an outline of how you see the character
b   how you'd like them to play the part
c   ideas for costume, movement and gesture
d   suggestions on how to deliver certain key lines.

73

6

Plot and structure

How does Shakespeare take the audience on a journey in *Macbeth*?

Your progress in this unit:
- understand and explain the structure of the plot
- interpret the theatricality and dramatic impact of the play
- explore how the action of the play develops
- write about plot and structure.

THE PLOT OF *MACBETH*

The story of a play is often referred to as its plot. *Macbeth*'s plot charts the rise and fall of Macbeth – a loyal nobleman and soldier who becomes the murderous and tyrannical king of Scotland after acting on the prophecies of three Witches whom he meets on a heath when returning from battle. The play follows the formal conventions of **tragedy** and questions who is responsible for Macbeth's actions.

The real Macbeth

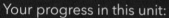

Macbeth is probably set in the 11th century – hundreds of years before Shakespeare wrote the play. At this time, a real king named Macbeth ruled Scotland while Edward the Confessor was king of England. In the play, Malcolm flees from Macbeth's tyranny to the court of the English king.

Shakespeare based *Macbeth* on information from Raphael Holinshed's *Chronicles of England, Scotland and Ireland*, a mixture of history and legend that was published in 1587. According to the *Chronicles*, Macbeth reigned for ten years.

Although there are no clear markers by which an audience can measure the passage of time in the play, Shakespeare seems to reduce events to the space of a few months. This contributes to the pace and drama of *Macbeth*.

THEATRICAL AND DRAMATIC STRUCTURE

Many features of *Macbeth* are consistent with Shakespeare's other plays as well as the theatrical conventions of the time. The play is split into five acts, but this was probably not obvious in early performances, and the acts may not have been marked in the staging script. It is likely that they were added to the published versions so that *Macbeth* conformed to the structure of 'classical' plays, as well as to make the progress of events clearer.

Although it was not clearly divided into acts in Shakespeare's day, there would certainly have been at least one break in the performance – just as there often is in productions today. This allowed the audience to eat and to enjoy the other forms of entertainment on show around the theatre sites, such as betting on animal fights.

The pace of the action

The acts and scenes in *Macbeth* are a variety of lengths. Some acts have a number of short scenes with a lot of fast-paced action, such as the opening scenes of Act 1. Other acts have fewer, longer scenes in which **characters** engage in extended **dialogue**. Act 4 Scene 3 – one of only three scenes in this act – is the longest in the play.

There may be less action in these scenes and the pace of the performance can seem slow, but the longer scenes provide details, explanations and additional information. Act 4 Scene 1, for example, is very dramatic – filled with Witches, apparitions and prophecies – but the action does not move forward so an audience may feel that nothing is happening. However, this scene is important in helping us understand Macbeth's state of mind and the terrible depths to which his ambition has brought him.

Shakespeare also varies the mood of the scenes, including some **comedy** so that the audience is not completely overwhelmed by tragedy early on in the play. The use of the comic Porter in Act 2 softens the effect of Duncan's murder. The humour in the early parts of the play also heightens the impact of Macbeth's horrific actions later on. Shakespeare also liked to **juxtapose** tragedy and comedy to intensify the effect of each.

THE STRUCTURE OF A TRAGEDY

The structure of a play can be explored in a number of different ways. For example you might comment upon any of the following aspects of structure in:

- the order of the scenes and the events
- the development of a character, a **theme** or an idea
- patterns of **verse**, dialogue or grammar.

The order of events in many plays and films, including tragedies, follows a three-stage pattern:

The **exposition** is the early part of the play. Here the audience learns who the main characters are and what they want out of life.

The **development** is the middle part of the play. This is where lots of things happen, leading to some kind of climax or conflict.

The **resolution** is the final part. It shows the outcome of the conflict and the fate of the main characters.

 Key terms

comedy: a play that is usually light-hearted and has a happy ending.

dialogue: a conversation between two or more people in a piece of writing.

Stay you imperfect speakers. Tell me more.

Macbeth: Act 1 Scene 3, line 68

DEVELOP AND REVISE

Developing a tragedy

1 Look at the following information. The typical exposition, development and resolution of a tragedy are shown. List those events in *Macbeth* that you think match this structure. The first example has been started for you.

Exposition	Development	Resolution
• We learn about the characters, setting and context. • We learn about the conflict that might occur and the secret weakness of the tragic hero.	• The tragic hero is at their most powerful. • But the secret weakness undermines them more and more. • Their enemies plot against them.	• The enemies reach full strength and defeat the tragic hero. • The tragic hero understands what has happened and understands their secret weakness. • The tragic hero dies, the survivors briefly comment and reflect.
We hear about Macbeth's success in battle (Act 1 Scene 2). We see his response to the Witches (Act 1 Scene 2).		

Write a mini-saga

2 A mini-saga takes a long story and reduces it to exactly 50 words (not including the title). It concludes with a five-word sentence and uses no more than three full stops in total. A mini-saga about the *Titanic* might be:

 Watch some actors summarise *Macbeth* in five freeze frames on Cambridge Elevate.

When she set sail from Southampton in 1912, they said that she was unsinkable, but on the maiden voyage to New York, an iceberg ripped that claim to pieces. Lifeboats for rich women and children, but over a thousand died in the ice cold waters.

And the band played on.

The history of Macbeth was originally presented as a concise entry in Holinshed's *Chronicles*, but Shakespeare greatly expanded the story. Can you cut it back down? Write a mini-saga telling Macbeth's story in 50 words.

Create a tragi-ometer

3 Shakespeare balances the scenes in the play to ensure that the horrors of Macbeth's actions are believable and do not overwhelm the audience.

Draw a graph similar to the example shown, to gauge which scenes introduce tragic elements and which include comedy. The mark shows the slightly tragic element of Act 1 Scene 1. Place additional marks higher or lower to show the change from scene to scene so that you can see the 'shape' of the action across the play. Can you see any patterns? Why might this be the case?

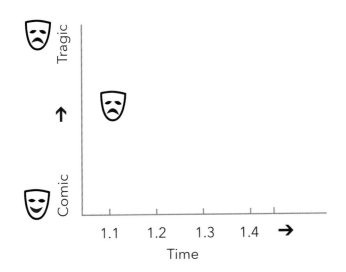

Untangle the plots

4 Being able to see how Shakespeare has woven the play's plots together will help you understand its complexity and the skill that the playwright demonstrates in telling the story effectively.

Use sticky notes in different colours. Choose a different colour for each plot element in the play. For example:

a   effect of the **supernatural**
b   Macbeth – rise and fall
c   Macbeth's relationships
d   kingship
e   tragedy.

Read through the play and, when you come across a detail relating to a particular plot, write down the act, scene and line reference, alongside a brief description and/or a key quotation that summarises what it adds to that plot. Use the examples from Act 1 below as a starting point.

When you have finished, rearrange the notes to group together all those that refer to a particular plot. This will allow you to estimate how much time or attention Shakespeare gave individual plot elements.

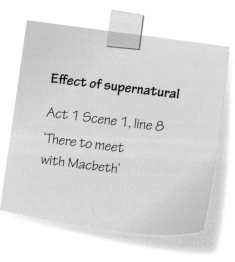

Effect of supernatural

Act 1 Scene 1, line 8
'There to meet
with Macbeth'

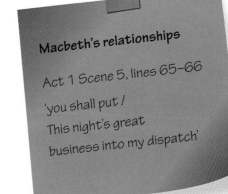

Macbeth's relationships

Act 1 Scene 5, lines 65–66

'you shall put /
This night's great
business into my dispatch'

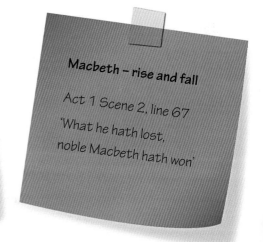

Macbeth – rise and fall

Act 1 Scene 2, line 67
'What he hath lost,
noble Macbeth hath won'

7

Context, setting and stagecraft

How does Shakespeare bring the characters and the action alive?

Your progress in this unit:
- understand and explore the context and setting of Macbeth
- understand how audiences would have watched and understood *Macbeth* in Shakespeare's time
- explore the ways in which action and change can be presented on stage.

CONTEXT AND SETTING

An audience watching one of Shakespeare's plays at the Globe Theatre in the 17th century would have had quite a different experience to someone watching a modern production.

The importance of the supernatural in the play

The opening scene of *Macbeth*, in which the Witches meet in a thunderstorm, is something of a shock to an audience. Some critics believe that it was added later and that Shakespeare's original play began with Act 1 Scene 2. How well do you think Scene 1 begins the story and introduces the **themes** that develop throughout the play? In what ways would the audience's experience of the play be different if it began with the entrance of the king and his court, and the arrival of the wounded Captain (Act 1 Scene 2)?

In fact, some people have questioned whether the play needs the Witches at all. A modern play or film about intense ambition and the sacrifices

Fact file

- Plays were usually performed outdoors.
- Plays generally started at 2 p.m.
- Recorded sound had not been invented.
- Electric lighting had not been invented.
- Many audience members stood on the stage.
- All the actors were men.
- There were not many opportunities for scene changes or heavy props.
- The most valuable items in the theatre were the costumes the actors wore.
- Very few audience members would have ever left London; hardly any would have left England.
- The thrones of England and Scotland had very recently been unified.
- Many people believed in witchcraft and it was punishable by death and eternal damnation.
- England had experienced numerous threats of invasion and rebellion in recent years.

made to become king, president or prime minister is unlikely to include **supernatural** beings. Macbeth could have been driven purely by his own ambition. He could have discussed with his wife not a prophecy, but Duncan's old age. He is the king's cousin: how little now stands between him and the throne! How can they just make sure that the old man …

Scotland and England

When Shakespeare wrote *Macbeth*, England and Scotland had recently been united under one crown, when King James VI of Scotland inherited the throne of England. They may have had one king, but England and Scotland were still separate countries, each with its own parliament.

When Malcolm flees to England in Act 2 Scene 3, he is going to a foreign country. His flight could be seen as treachery and a sign of guilt of Duncan's murder. Macbeth certainly claims this in Act 3 when he says:

> In England and in Ireland, not confessing
> Their cruel parricide, filling their hearers
> With strange invention.

Macbeth: Act 3 Scene 1, lines 32–34

Here, Macbeth is a Scottish king in Scotland, commenting on events in England. Mirroring this, an audience in the early 17th century would comprise English people in London watching events in *Macbeth*'s Scotland.

STAGECRAFT, THEATRICALITY AND PERFORMANCE

Putting on a performance

In drama, writing is aimed at performance. And performance is best when it involves surprise, variety and contrast. Surprise is a matter of plot. Variety can involve a mix of **comedy** and passion and **tragedy**, appealing to all possible tastes in the audience. It is also to do with mixing action, song, dance, spectacle – pleasing the audience through the eyes and the ears. Theatricality is the ability to fill an evening in the theatre with enough to keep the audience interested and entertained.

Shakespeare began his working life as an actor, so he knew what actors needed from a script to be able to perform on stage. He knew they must have cues so they knew when to speak and move. Shakespeare also knew that he could use different methods to create interesting effects, such as having **characters** hiding on parts of the stage or dressing people up so other characters did not recognise them or using language so the audience knew a scene took place in darkness.

Watch a video about an unusual performance of *Macbeth* on Cambridge Elevate.

79

Staging battles

One of the biggest decisions directors have to make when staging *Macbeth* is how to show the complex battle sequences. Some choose to begin the play by showing the battle with Macdonald's forces (which Shakespeare does not include). The final scenes show Macbeth's downfall in battle, and most directors try to make these as dramatic as possible in order to leave a strong impression on their audience at the end of the play. Modern productions sometimes depict Macbeth's death in a very graphic way and in the final scene, Shakespeare has Macduff enter the stage carrying Macbeth's head.

The challenge of change

The historic Macbeth reigned for 17 years, but the play about him is one of Shakespeare's shortest. In such a short time span, Macbeth's rise and fall can seem unreal if the director and designer do not take steps to show change and contrast in the final act.

Some productions aim to show the changes in the character of Macbeth through use of make-up, costume and the actions and facial gestures of the actor playing Macbeth. In one production, Macbeth's costume became more untidy and he became more stooped to show his downfall. In another production, the appearance of the actor became wilder, with piercing, staring eyes that were accentuated with black and red make-up.

SHAKESPEARE THE DRAMATIST

Shakespeare wrote *Macbeth*, like all his plays, as a public entertainment. His scripts are designed to be performed. For example Shakespeare wants the audience to feel suspense as Macbeth and Lady Macbeth speak after the murder. He uses short lines, with questions used to express urgency and uncertainty. These lines provide cues to help the actors to speak the lines, to perform actions with the lines, and to show a changing relationship after the murder has been carried out:

Lady Macbeth:	My husband?
Macbeth:	I have done the deed. Didst thou not hear a noise?
Lady Macbeth:	I heard an owl scream and the crickets cry. Did not you speak?
Macbeth:	When?
Lady Macbeth:	Now.
Macbeth:	As I descended?
Lady Macbeth:	Ay.
Macbeth:	Hark, who lies i'th'second chamber?
Lady Macbeth:	Donaldbain.
Macbeth:	This is a sorry sight.
Lady Macbeth:	A foolish thought, to say a sorry sight.

Macbeth: Act 2 Scene 2, lines 13–24

DEVELOP AND REVISE

Understanding performances in Shakespeare's day

1 Look back at the fact file on conditions in Shakespeare's day. For each fact, think about how it might have created **challenges** and **opportunities** for a production of *Macbeth*. Create a table to record your answers.

Fact	Challenge	Opportunity
Plays were usually performed outdoors.	How do you convincingly create a dark and stormy atmosphere on a sunny afternoon?	Allows a focus on the descriptive language; the use of music, gestures and voice would make up for it.

The importance of the opening

2 The play starts with the appearance of three Witches arranging to meet: '**When shall we three meet again**?'. Look at the following statements, giving some reasons why Shakespeare might have chosen to start the play in this way. In small groups, discuss each reason and decide on their order of importance.

   a   Shakespeare wanted to shock the audience into silence at the start.

   b   Shakespeare wanted to appeal to James I, who was interested in witches.

   c   The Witches' appearance sets the evil tone for the play and suggest that bad things will happen.

   d   People enjoy watching the supernatural and Shakespeare wanted to excite his audience.

   e   The Witches represent the evil of characters in the play, such as the Macbeths.

Design a stage set

3 In Act 4 Scene 3, England under King Edward contrasts with Scotland under Macbeth. Consider how you would show this contrast to the audience. Draw a set design of the stage for this scene. Label it with details of how it provides a contrast to the Scotland scenes that the audience will have seen previously. Explain the effect that you are trying to create.

Plan a performance

4 Imagine you are about to direct a production of *Macbeth*. Make notes on how you would use stagecraft, theatricality and performance to engage your audience. For example which offstage events in Act 1 would you show? (Macbeth killing Macdonald? The Thane of Cawdor's execution?).

Include notes for your stage manager explaining how you intend to stage the act. How would you show the action using modern technical methods and lighting/sound effects? Use the following statements to guide your note-making:

   a   I would 'hook' the audience by …

   b   The audience should be surprised by …

   c   I would try to create a … atmosphere by …

   d   The most challenging technical aspect would be …

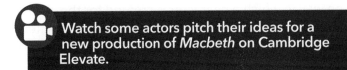

Watch some actors pitch their ideas for a new production of *Macbeth* on Cambridge Elevate.

When shall we three meet again?

First Witch: Act 1 Scene 1, line 1

8

Character and characterisation

How does Shakespeare create such dramatic characters?

Your progress in this unit:
- understand and explore the characters in the play
- interpret how the characters represent ideas and attitudes
- explore the ways in which Shakespeare presents these characters
- analyse the changes in certain characters through the play
- write about character and characterisation.

THE CREATION OF CHARACTERS

The way in which a character is created for the audience is called **characterisation**. We learn most about the **characters** from the words Shakespeare wrote for his actors. However, he also builds up information about his characters in other ways, including the use of **stage directions**.

Reported behaviour

A recurring pattern in *Macbeth* is the way that Shakespeare develops the audience's impression of a character – particularly Macbeth – through the words he gives the characters. In Act 1, for example, details of Macbeth's actions are reported to Duncan, so that before we have even met Macbeth we know that he is '**brave**' and '**noble**', and that he is a fearless and skilful warrior. Shakespeare also uses this device in Act 5: without seeing the actions ourselves, we know that he has become a '**tyrant**' who others fear is '**mad**', who cannot control his government '**Within the belt of rule**' and who commits '**secret murders**'.

Use of soliloquy

Throughout the play, certain characters share their thoughts directly with the audience in **soliloquies**. This allows the audience to see that the private thoughts of the characters are sometimes at odds with what they do and say in public. In Act 1 Scene 3, lines 126–141, for example, we witness Macbeth's confused thoughts as the Witches' prophecies start to come true. To a degree, Shakespeare involves and implicates the audience in Macbeth's actions by sharing his thoughts in this way.

CHARACTER DEVELOPMENT

In any work of fiction, characters that are all good or all bad are less convincing than those who demonstrate both good and bad features, or who change over the course of a narrative. Most good people occasionally do something bad, and even wicked people may sometimes turn out to have some good qualities.

Showing a character's psychological and moral complexity is one of Shakespeare's greatest skills as a playwright. As the play develops, so do the actions and words of the characters. For example Macbeth's initial doubts about the steps he must take to win more power disappear after the first few murders. At times it seems that Shakespeare wants to plant a seed of doubt about whether a character is truly evil.

Near the end of the play, when Macbeth's reign of terror is at its height, he gives a speech beginning '**Tomorrow, and tomorrow, and tomorrow**' which demonstrates a rare moment of humanity, suggesting that beneath his evil exterior, Macbeth remains a complex character. This speech, delivered just before Macbeth's downfall, may change an audience's reaction to his death. It makes us think more deeply about all sides to the character rather than simply cheering the death of tyrant.

INTERPRETING CHARACTER

Characters representing attitudes and ideas

Shakespeare generally avoids using **stereotypes** – characters that simply represent an idea or attitude. In *Macbeth*, the Witches are an example of this type of character, bringing a sense of darkness and evil to the play. However, Shakespeare sets up many of the other characters to contrast with each other in order to guide the audience's impression of them. He also reveals new aspects of characters as the play develops, to make them appear more well-rounded and therefore more believable.

Key terms

stereotype: an oversimplified but common image or idea of a particular person or thing.

Tomorrow, and tomorrow, and tomorrow
Creeps in this petty pace from day to day
To the last syllable of recorded time

Macbeth: Act 5 Scene 5, lines 18–20

Characters in contrast

Several characters are used to provide a contrast with Macbeth. They remain convincing characters in their own right, but the way in which Shakespeare juxtaposes them allows the audience to draw comparisons and to determine their strengths and their failings.

In Act 1, the (unseen) Thane of Cawdor provides an early contrast to Macbeth, showing him to be a skilful warrior and a man of honour. In Act 2, Shakespeare uses the words and actions of Banquo to contrast with those of Macbeth and show the change in his character. First Banquo rejects the Witches' prophecies, despite the suggestion that he will benefit from them, while Macbeth chooses to believe the Witches' words. Then Banquo's ghost serves as a reminder of the lengths to which Macbeth will go to get what he wants.

Later, a contrast is drawn between the ambition of Macbeth and the loyalty of Macduff to the king of Scotland. This is further highlighted in Act 5, when the audience sees the immediate peace and order that Malcolm brings to Scotland on his return from exile.

Macduff's home life, and the love and loyalty shown to him by his wife and children, provides a strong contrast to the childless Macbeths and their complicated relationship. This may show how the Macbeths are uncaring and 'unnatural' in their attitude and behaviour.

PAGE VERSUS STAGE

The characters in Shakespeare's plays are only partly defined by the words he gives them. One of the reasons for Shakespeare's enduring popularity is that the words of his plays, the decisions of a director and the skill of an actor can be combined to interpret his characters in many different ways.

Casting characters

Deliberately casting actors who look similar in the parts of Macbeth and Macduff might emphasise the great differences in their characters despite a similarity in their looks. Equally, making them look **very** different could have the same effect. Particular actors also bring certain qualities to a role. Many famous actors have been cast as Macbeth and Lady Macbeth because of other roles they have played and the associations this could bring to the parts.

Historical characters

Some productions link Macbeth to real historical tyrants, dictators and despots through the use of costumes, expressions, actions and accents. This encourages the audience to interpret the characters on stage in the light of their knowledge of the real historical figures.

 Key terms

adverb: a word used to describe a verb or an adjective.

Behold where stands Th'usurper's cursèd head.

Macduff: Act 5 Scene 9, lines 21–22

DEVELOP AND REVISE

Write the stage directions

1 Choose one of the scenes that you are studying in detail and add stage directions in the modern manner:

a Add a description of the characters and explain how they enter and exit the stage.

b Put **adverbs** before each character's lines to show how the line should be said (e.g. 'cheerfully', 'threateningly'). Use brackets to show the actor where the direction begins and ends.

2 When you have finished your scene, work with others who have written stage directions for the same scene and act out each one. How do the different stage directions affect the characterisation in the scene?

Chart the developments

3 Being able to visualise the changes in a character throughout the course of a play will give you an appreciation of Shakespeare's skill in making his characters believable. You can do this by charting an aspect of the character on a plot and line graph – for example Macbeth's actions and intentions to others, as shown in the red line below.

Copy the graph and complete the first plot and line section. Add other plots and lines that chart Macbeth's ambition and his state of mind.

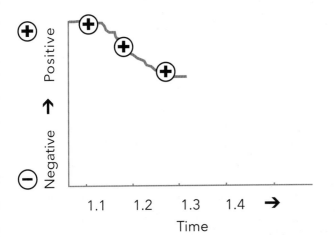

Develop this task by adding quotations to support your decisions in where to place the points in the graph. What conclusions can you draw from the graph? For example does a positive change have a negative impact elsewhere in Macbeth's character?

4 Create a second plot and line graph to show the development in Lady Macbeth's character. How does her graph compare to Macbeth's?

5 Choose another character from *Macbeth*. Create a montage of images that represent your chosen character throughout the play. You could choose pictures showing different actors, or scenes from the same production with the same actor, to show the changes in the character in each scene.

Contrast connections

6 Write a list of the main characters in *Macbeth*, then find pictures for each character. Use these to visualise the web of connections, comparisons and contrasts in the play. In the example, a red line suggests a contrast and green a connection. Write on the lines to explain the links. Use quotations if you can.

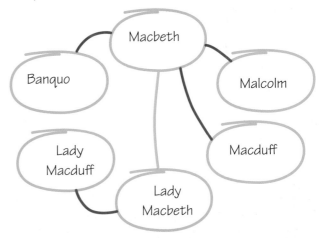

7 As an extension to this activity, produce a different connection web for each of the five acts in the play to show how the relationships and contracts change.

 Watch Macbeth and Lady Macbeth reflect on their actions on Cambridge Elevate.

9

Ideas, perspectives and themes

What are the big ideas that dominate *Macbeth*?

Your progress in this unit:
- understand and explore the major ideas in the play
- interpret how these themes are communicated to an audience
- explore different interpretations of and perspectives on the play
- research and write about themes in the play.

WHAT IS THE MESSAGE OF *MACBETH*?

Shakespeare did not write his plays to be studied in schools and colleges, or written about in exams, or even read in a book. He expected them to be watched and heard in the theatre. But *Macbeth* is a rich play, and your understanding and enjoyment of it can be enhanced by exploring its important **themes**.

Over the centuries, people have expressed many different ideas about the message of *Macbeth* and how it should be expressed on stage. Some people believe this is a deeply political play – about leadership and the qualities that make a good king. Others think that the morality of murder is the key element of the play. Some productions present Macbeth in a sympathetic way; others focus on the recurring violence. What do you think is the most important idea or message in *Macbeth*?

MAJOR THEMES IN *MACBETH*

Although no two interpretations of the play will be the same, most experts agree that Shakespeare had certain themes on his mind as he wrote. Six of these are discussed in this unit, but you will come across others in your study of *Macbeth*. In an exam, discussing the themes will help you demonstrate your understanding of the play as a whole, as they are intrinsically linked to other key features. For example when writing about the character of Macbeth, you will need to discuss the theme of ambition in the play.

Ambition

The ambitions of Macbeth and his wife make them ruthless, powerful and destructive. Ambition can be thought of as the tragic flaw that leads to his downfall.

Look at these quotations in which the theme of ambition can be identified:

> I am Thane of Cawdor.
> If good, why do I yield to that suggestion
> Whose horrid image doth unfix my hair

Macbeth: Act 1 Scene 3, lines 132–134

> Thy letters have transported me beyond
> This ignorant present, and I feel now
> The future in the instant.

Lady Macbeth: Act 1 Scene 5, lines 54–56

> I have no spur
> To prick the sides of my intent, but only
> Vaulting ambition which o'erleaps itself

Macbeth: Act 1 Scene 7, lines 25-27

> I dare do all that may become a man;
> Who dares do more is none.

Macbeth: Act 1 Scene 7, lines 46-47

> What hath quenched them, hath given me fire.

Lady Macbeth: Act 2 Scene 2, line 2

> To be thus is nothing,
> But to be safely thus.

Macbeth: Act 3 Scene 1, lines 49-50

The last of these comes from Macbeth's **soliloquy** in Act 3, in which he identifies Banquo as a threat. He concludes that achieving the crown is only worthwhile if he can retain it: **'to be safely thus'**. This shows Macbeth's ambition, ruthlessness and fear: he cannot rest until all threats are eliminated.

There are different ways of interpreting the Macbeths' ambition. Some critics argue that the influence of the Witches is central to their actions. Others emphasise the personal ambition of Macbeth and Lady Macbeth, arguing that the prophecies merely exploit their personal **'vaulting'** ambition.

When considering whether Macbeth's actions are the consequence of meeting the Witches, whether his wife pushes him into violence or whether he was ambitious all along, you will need to show how different interpretations are possible. You should also support your ideas with quotations from the play.

Appearance and reality

Things are rarely as they seem in *Macbeth*. From the very first scene (**'Fair is foul, and foul is fair'**), the idea that the natural order of things cannot be trusted is fixed in our minds. **Characters** are deceitful and hypocritical – they tell lies. For example Lady Macbeth offers King Duncan a warm welcome to her home when she is already plotting his murder. When Banquo reminds Macbeth of the Witches' prophecy in Act 2 Scene 1, Macbeth claims to have given their words no thought, when the reality is that he can think of little else.

In addition to this, several characters in *Macbeth* experience visions, and the boundaries between dreams and reality is blurred as natural, unnatural and **supernatural** events unfold. All these elements provide challenges to the director, who must decide how to help the audience distinguish between appearance and reality.

Thy letters have transported me beyond This ignorant present

Lady Macbeth: Act 1 Scene 5, lines 54-55

Good and evil

This blood-soaked play is a study of the evil humans are capable of showing towards one another. But the play also explores the idea of supernatural evil. For example the Witches' influence on Macbeth proves to be devastating. These creatures haunt the play, summoning foul weather and foul visions, infecting the story with a dark and sinister atmosphere.

The element of witchcraft can be included in a discussion of good and evil in the play, but you should also consider other examples of this theme. Many evil crimes are committed, including several murders. There are also many examples of goodness, and characters who show honour and loyalty. When writing about characters, speeches, actions and scenes, make sure you consider **in what way** they are good or evil – or a mixture of both.

Order and chaos

Macbeth opens with the chaos of war. In the course of the play, the audience witnesses destruction, murder and oppression. The world is turned upside down, and unnatural and cruel events become commonplace as Macbeth's violent journey turns him into Scotland's tyrant.

However, it also begins and ends with a **good** king – Duncan and Malcolm, respectively. This might be a play about chaos and destruction, but it is also about order and restoration. Shakespeare was fascinated by kingship and the importance of the king to the health of a country and many critics believe he was sending a message to his own king, James I. What do you think?

Other themes

Gender is another important theme in Macbeth, and there are several places where the gender of a character influences events:

- Macbeth is accused of being unmanly (and defends himself).
- Lady Macbeth asks to be unsexed (having talked about babies, breastfeeding and infanticide).
- Banquo comments that the Witches have beards.
- The Witches worship a goddess.

The natural world becoming unnatural is also recurring idea in the play. For example:

- **Nature:** the wounded captain makes the first reference in Act 1 Scene 2.
- **Unnatural:** an Old Man makes the first reference.
- **Supernatural:** the word itself does not appear in the play, but plenty of things happen that could be described that way. What qualities do they share?

Tyrant, show thy face!

Macduff: Act 5 Scene 7, line 15

DEVELOP AND REVISE

Separate the real from the unreal

1 To help you more fully understand the theme of appearance and reality, draw a table with two columns with these words as headings. Find some key quotations from the play and write them in one of the columns, according to where you feel they best belong.

Identify good and evil

2 Look at the following scenes. Identify the words or short phrases that **connote** evil or the supernatural. Some examples have been given to start you off. Once you have a list, consider what the different words and phrases have in common.

3 In Act 5 Scene 7, Macduff shouts out for Macbeth in the chaos of battle: '**Tyrant, show thy face!**' Write a list of ten ways in which you think Macbeth shows the face of a tyrant throughout the play.

Support the themes with quotations

4 Copy and complete the following statements, adding detail in the form of relevant quotations:

a   Act 1 balances the themes of order and chaos. For example … .

b   Macbeth's tyranny is perhaps most obvious when he … .

c   A sense of chaos is created in Act 2 by the way … .

d   In Act 2 Scene 3, Lennox seems to hint at the chaos that is about to be unleashed on Scotland when … .

e   In Act 2 Scene 4, the Old Man and Ross discuss how unnatural events and chaos are taking place in Scotland … .

f   In Act 3 Scene 1, Macbeth's tyranny is shown by … .

g   Shakespeare demonstrates that Lady Macbeth is essential to Macbeth's tyranny by … .

h   Act 4 renews the theme of order by … .

i   In Act 5, Lady Macbeth's mind has descended into chaos. For example … .

Scene	Evil or supernatural references
Act 1 Scene 1	
Act 1 Scene 3	
Act 2 Scene 1	'The bell invites me' 'Witchcraft celebrates'
Act 3 Scene 4	
Act 3 Scene 5	
Act 4 Scene 1	'poisoned entrails' 'for a charm of powerful trouble' 'Something wicked this way comes'
Act 5 Scene 7	
Act 5 Scene 8	

10
Language

Why do the language and actions in *Macbeth* carry such impact?

Your progress in this unit:
- analyse and explore language across the whole play
- explore and interpret links between character and language
- identify and analyse common images or features of language
- write about Shakespeare's use of language.

LANGUAGE IN SHAKESPEARE'S WORLD

Shakespeare's plays reflect the changing attitudes of the time in which he lived. As society distanced itself from the influence of the Catholic Church, it also rejected its image-based methods of storytelling – statues, paintings and enactments of Bible stories, such as the medieval mystery plays. Instead, Protestant society under Elizabeth I and James I focused more on the Bible and the power of the word. Shakespeare's language, therefore, is a significant feature of his plays.

Finding the words

Shakespeare mixes the language of the upper classes with the bawdy language he heard in the inns where some of his plays were performed. Compare Duncan's eloquent language in Act 1 Scene 2, for example, with the Porter's foul language and **innuendo** in Act 2 Scene 3 to see how Shakespeare draws language from many sources. He chooses the language for each of his **characters** carefully, as it signals how an audience should respond to them.

Early modern English

Shakespeare uses what is technically called 'Early Modern English'. As English has changed during 400 years, his language can sometimes be difficult for people today to understand. A good edition of the play provides explanations of difficult words or phrases. However, there are some features that are confusing. For example, 'you', 'your' and 'yours' can be expressed in a number of ways:

Thou	'You'	'Glamis thou art, and Cawdor, and shalt be / What thou art promised' (Act 1 Scene 5, lines 13–14)
Thee	'You'	'Come, thick night, / And pall thee in the dunnest smoke of hell' (Act 1 Scene 5, lines 48–49)
Ye	'You'	'Are ye fantastical, or that indeed / Which outwardly ye show?' (Act 1 Scene 3, lines 51–52)
Thy	'Your'	'From this time, / Such I account thy love' (Act 1 Scene 7, lines 38–39)
Thine	'Your'	'Art thou afeared / To be the same in thine own act and valour / And thou art in desire?' (Act 1 Scene 7, lines 39–41)

IMAGERY

Imagination was very important to audiences at the Globe Theatre, Blackfriars Theatre, and the inns, great houses and palaces where *Macbeth* would have been performed. In Shakespeare's time, there were few special effects available. The Globe Theatre did not even have lighting and, with limited scenery, actors had to rely on the physical characteristics of the performance space to set the scene. The words spoken by the characters were also essential in revealing location and suggesting the passing of time. For example in Act 2 Scene 1, a Shakespearean audience would understand that Banquo and Fleance are meeting at night not because of a change in stage lighting, but because Banquo greets his son with the words: '**How goes the night, boy?**'

The use of words to mark where and when action takes place can be difficult for a modern audience used to the more visual storytelling of television and films. However, Shakespeare's language is rich in **imagery**, which draws in the audience, stirs the imagination, deepens dramatic impact and gives insight into character.

Imagery in Macbeth

Images of blood recur throughout the play. It begins and ends with bloody battles and is punctuated with murders. It is her sleepwalking obsession with ridding her hands of bloodstains that drives Lady Macbeth to her death. After the appearance of Banquo's ghost at the feast and his realisation that Macduff has turned against him, Macbeth vows to carry on committing murders and carrying out evil deeds with the words:

I am in blood
Stepped in so far that I should wade no more,
Returning were as tedious as go o'er.

Macbeth: Act 3 Scene 4, lines 136–138

Other recurring images in *Macbeth* include:

- **darkness:** much of the action takes place at night and the images of darkness give an impression of evil and the supernatural
- **theatre:** there are references to playing a part and only having a short time to achieve something significant (e.g. Macbeth's speech when he hears of Lady Macbeth's death in Act 5 Scene 5)
- **disease:** recurring images of pestilence suggests evil, and disease was often thought of as a punishment for sin ('**filthy air**', Lady Macbeth's '**mind diseased**')
- **animals:** images of ferocious creatures occur throughout the play, heightening the threatening atmosphere (e.g. Macbeth describes his mind as '**full of scorpions**').

 Key terms

innuendo: a hint or suggestion, usually a negative one.

Canst thou not minister to a mind diseased

Macbeth: Act 5 Scene 3, line 41

VERSE AND PROSE

According to the conventions of the time, tragedies such as *Macbeth* recounted the affairs of rulers and leaders. This means that most characters are high-status and therefore speak in verse, particularly blank verse. A Jacobean audience would have expected the characters of kings and thanes to speak in this way, especially in scenes that were especially dramatic or emotional. Prose (the way people normally speak) was typically used for low-status characters and comic scenes.

Shakespeare did not always stick to these conventions and there are points in *Macbeth* where he bends the rules in subtly dramatic ways. In Act 2, for example, the low-status, worldly-wise Porter uses prose. Unusually, when Macduff and Lennox – both high-status characters – join him, they also switch to prose. In Act 5, the Doctor and Gentlewoman also speak mostly in prose. However, when they are under scrutiny they switch to verse.

This change in language gives the audience more information about the characters. It also helps the actors understand how the scenes should be played and the lines delivered. Prose will be more natural and informal, whereas the rhythm of verse results in a more formal delivery, making a character seem more authoritative.

 Watch a video about Shakespeare's language on Cambridge Elevate.

REPETITION AND ANTITHESIS

Shakespeare often chooses words for their sound quality as well as their meaning, and enjoys using repetition to add pace and tension to a scene:

First Witch: Show!
Second Witch: Show!
Third Witch: Show!
All the Witches: Show his eyes and grieve his heart

Act 4 Scene 1, lines 106–109

Repetition is also used to emphasise an idea, as a single word is repeated again and again:

Though you untie the winds and let them fight
Against the churches, though the yeasty waves
Confound and swallow navigation up,
Though bladed corn be lodged and trees blown
    down
Though castles topple on their warders' heads,
Though palaces and pyramids do slope
Their heads to their foundations, though the
    treasure
Of nature's germen tumble altogether
Even till destruction sicken

Macbeth: Act 4 Scene 1, lines 51–59

Antithesis is also used effectively in *Macbeth* to show the clash of good and evil and reflect the breakdown of the natural order:

When the battle's lost, and won.

Second Witch: Act 1 Scene 1, line 4

Fair is foul, and foul is fair

All Witches: Act 1 Scene 1, line 12

 Key terms

antithesis: two opposite ideas that are put together to achieve a contrasting effect.

DEVELOP AND REVISE

Find the words

1 On the internet you can find applications that will analyse a section of text to make the frequently recurring words stand out in a larger and bolder font. Choose a section from *Macbeth* and paste it into one of these applications. The larger and bolder words will help you to identify the words that are used frequently to create the imagery.

  a Are you surprised by the words that stand out in the section of text?

  b What do these words tell you about the scene that you analysed, the characters involved and the play as a whole?

  c Which words do certain characters say most and least?

Private prose

2 Macbeth is mostly written in verse, but occasionally Shakespeare removes the barrier between performers and spectators and has his characters speak in ordinary prose like his audience would. Study the moments when characters in the play speak in prose:

  * Macbeth's letter in Act 1 Scene 5
  * the Porter's monologue in Act 2 Scene 3
  * the conversation between Lady Macduff and her son in Act 4 Scene 2
  * the conversation between the Doctor and the Gentlewoman, and Lady Macbeth's sleepwalking speeches in Act 5 Scene 1.

  a Why do you think the characters switch from verse to prose?

  b What is the effect on the audience?

  c What might Shakespeare be suggesting about the characters by changing the form of their language?

Recurring themes

3 As you read the play, note down the key quotations on the following language **themes**:

  a darkness
  b blood
  c nature
  d animals and beasts
  e the theatre.

4 When you have finished, choose a different colour per theme and highlight the quotations in each act thematically. This will help you spot developments and changes in the language as the play progresses. For example are there more quotations about darkness later in the play? Do particular characters use a particular theme more frequently than others? If so, what does it say about them?

5 Choose one word or phrase that you feel best sums up each of the language themes you have studied.

Fair is foul, and foul is fair

All Witches: Act 1 Scene 1, line 12

Preparing for your exam

Your progress in this unit:
- understand what the exam requires and the skills you need to show
- prepare for your exam by planning and responding to a practice question
- assess your skills against example responses to the question
- improve your skills in writing for GCSE English Literature.

What the exam requires

For your GCSE English Literature, you will be assessed on *Macbeth* in **Section A** of **Paper 1: Shakespeare and the 19th-century novel**.
You will have 1 hour and 45 minutes to complete Paper 1 and it is worth 40% of your GCSE English Literature. You have just over 50 minutes for your answer on *Macbeth*.

You will have to answer one question on *Macbeth*. You will be required to write in detail about an extract from the play that is printed on your exam paper and then to write about the play as a whole. The question is worth 30 marks.

The assessment objective skills

Your answers will be assessed against four assessment objectives (AOs) – skills that you are expected to show. These are shown in full in the 'Introducing *Macbeth*' section and are outlined below in relationship to your responses. Notice the marks for each assessment objective and take account of this as you manage your time and focus your response.

- **AO1:** Read, understand and write about what happens in the play, referring to the text and using relevant quotations (12 marks).
- **AO2:** Analyse the language, form and structure used by Shakespeare to create meanings and effects (12 marks).
- **AO3:** Show an understanding of the context of the play. This might include, depending on the question, when Shakespeare wrote the play, the period in which he set the play and why, its relevance to audiences then and to you in the 21st century (6 marks).
- **AO4:** Use a range of vocabulary and sentence structures for clarity, purpose and effect, with accurate spelling and punctuation (4 marks).

What to do in the exam

- At the beginning of the exam, spend some time looking very carefully at the question. Make sure you understand exactly what you are being asked to do.
- Annotate the extract and plan what you want to write about for the extract and about the play as a whole.

Read the practice question and the annotations.

Macbeth

Read the following extract from Act 1 Scene 5 of *Macbeth* and then answer the question that follows.

At this point in the play Lady Macbeth is speaking. She has just received the news that King Duncan will be spending the night at her castle.

> The raven himself is hoarse
> That croaks the fatal entrance of Duncan
> Under my battlements. Come, you spirits
> That tend on mortal thoughts, unsex me here
> 5   And fill me from the crown to the toe topfull
> Of direst cruelty; make thick my blood,
> Stop up th'access and passage to remorse
> That no compunctious visitings of nature
> Shake my fell purpose nor keep peace between
> 10   Th'effect and it. Come to my woman's breasts,
> And take my milk for gall, you murd'ring ministers,
> Wherever in your sightless substances
> You wait on nature's mischief. Come, thick night,
> And pall thee in the dunnest smoke of hell,
> 15   That my keen knife see not the wound it makes,
> Nor heaven peep through the blanket of the dark,
> To cry, 'Hold, hold.'

Starting with this speech, explain how far you think Shakespeare presents Lady Macbeth as a powerful woman. Write about:

- how Shakespeare presents Lady Macbeth in this speech
- how Shakespeare presents Lady Macbeth in the play as a whole.

[30 marks]
AO4 [4 marks]

Annotations:

- bird associated with death
- onomatopoeia: sounds threatening
- she thinks of the castle as hers
- link with Witches?
- murderous plans
- is she a powerful woman?
- alliteration emphasises how complete the operation should be
- no pangs of conscience
- determined to murder
- my plan and the achievement of it
- a huge contrast with nurturing mother's milk
- alliterative; refers back to the spirits
- kept towards the end of the speech for dramatic effect
- she plans to do it!!
- This asks you for a 'response' to an idea, or statement, about an aspect of the play. (AO1)
- Focus on the writer to think about the text as created by Shakespeare. Remember that Lady Macbeth isn't a real person! (AO2)
- Start with a close reference to the text, on the printed extract, before widening your response to the play as a whole. (AO1, AO2)
- This asks you to think about contextual elements: in this case the idea of 'power' as well as ideas about women in this context. You need to stick to this topic. (AO3)
- Remember the sleepwalking scene and the report of Lady Macbeth's death later in the play. Remember it is your response. Use 'I think' in the conclusion.
- You need to make some sort of judgement here.
- The bullets remind you to focus on both the extract and the play as a whole.

Plan your answer

When planning your answer to any question, you should focus on three key areas:

- What do you know about the characters, events and ideas at this stage – in this extract and in the play as a whole? (AO1)
- What comments can you make about how Shakespeare uses language and style, using examples from this extract? (AO2)
- What is relevant in this extract that relates to the context of the play as a whole? (AO3)

Look at this example of a student's plan. Then explore the example paragraphs and development of skills in writing for GCSE English Literature that follow.

wants to be queen – asks to be unsexed

plans to commit the murder – 'My keen knife'

calls him a coward – 'When you durst do it, then you were a man.'

comes up with the plan (practical) – 'But screw your courage …'

immediately decides to kill Duncan

controls Macbeth

CONCLUSION powerful?

yes to start with – no at the end

POWERFUL WOMAN

is in control of murder – puts blood on grooms

would have killed Duncan but he looked like her father

washes off blood – 'a little water clears us of the deed'

BUT goes mad

quick-witted

tries to wash away the blood – 'Out, damned spot'

commits suicide?

faints as distraction when murder discovered

sorts out problem at banquet – 'a thing of custom'

- **The best answers** explore Shakespeare's craft and purpose in creating a character. They will connect what the character does to the writer's ideas and to the effects upon an audience watching. They offer a personal response and provide many well-explained details.
- **Good answers** show a clear understanding of how Shakespeare develops Lady Macbeth, using well-chosen examples.
- **Weaker answers** only explain what happens with Lady Macbeth without using many examples or mentioning how Shakespeare presents her.

Show your skills

To help you think about your own writing, look at these six example paragraphs of writing about Lady Macbeth. The annotations show the range of skills displayed in each paragraph.

Lady Macbeth wants the night to come so that she can kill King Duncan without anyone seeing her.

> some simple facts stated

Lady Macbeth wants the night to be really dark like hell so that heaven cannot see to stop her killing Duncan. This is a contrast of light (heaven) and dark (hell).

> statement supported with quotation

Lady Macbeth is determined to kill the king. I know this because she says 'my keen knife'. This means that her knife will have a very sharp blade and so she will be able to kill him quickly before anyone can stop her. Shakespeare uses the word 'keen' to emphasise how easily she will be able to kill Duncan. In fact she doesn't kill him because he looked like her father when he was asleep. She is also surprised at how much blood he had in him.

> explanation structured by reference to author, audience and other parts of the text

Shakespeare compares 'thick night' to 'the dunnest smoke of hell'. The idea of night being 'thick' means that nobody will be able to see through it and the comparison to hell shows that Lady Macbeth understands how evil she is planning to be.

> provides a range of details to keep clearly illustrating a point

Shakespeare uses the word 'peep' to describe the idea of heaven, which he personifies, looking through a blanket. 'Peep' implies having only a limited sight and looking at something quickly through a small opening. But even 'peeping' would show the dreadful nature of Lady Macbeth's crime.

> uses details to develop an interpretation going beyond what the text states explicitly

The final line in the soliloquy uses repetition to demonstrate the nature of her crime. The word 'cry' shows both pain and urgency: heaven, having only a slight sight of what she plans, is determined to stop her, even though she is shrouded in the smoke of hell – a hell the Porter will recognise in a scene that is both comic and horrific, and that demonstrates to the audience that Dunsinane has become a type of living hell. The contrast is an example of Shakespeare's exploration of the theme of deceit: nothing in the play is as it appears.

> an argued interpretation focused on writer, theatrical context and ideas

Plan and write your own response

Now plan and write your own response to the practice question.
You can then assess your skills against the example responses that follow.

ASSESS YOUR SKILLS

The following extracts are from sample responses to the practice question. They provide examples of skills at different levels when writing for GCSE English Literature. Use these examples to assess your own skills in responding to the practice question, so that you know what you do well and can focus on areas to improve. As you read the responses, think about how far each example – and your own answer – is successful in:

- using details from the text to support what the students have written
- using details to build up an interpretation of a character or a theme
- exploring Shakespeare's use of language and structure as well as his intentions in writing the play.

Student A

This is taken from the opening of Student A's response:

In her soliloquy Lady Macbeth is planning Duncan's murder. It seems that she and Macbeth have already discussed this and now they have their chance. She observes that the raven is hoarse and 'croaks'. This is onomatopoeia and shows the audience what noise a raven makes. People at the time thought that a raven was a messenger of death. So straightaway the audience would know that she meant to murder Duncan. She wants to stop being a woman and have her mother's milk replaced by a bitter poison. The audience realises that she is determined to be evil. She asks for the 'murd'ring ministers' to help her. This alliteration gives the phrase emphasis and means the audience will take special note of it. She wants 'thick night', which means that nobody will ever see the murder so nobody will ever find out the truth and they will get away with it. For the same reason she wants Heaven not to see what is going on. She is obviously evil and she seems to be very powerful. She also says that she is happy to commit the murder herself when she says 'my keen knife'.

uses technical term well

puts extract into a little context

two details from the text

identifies language technique with a little explanation

explanation of significance of raven

refers to text

explains effect on audience

direct quotation from extract

identifies effect

identifies language technique

explains quotations

starts to sustain ideas

links back to the question

This is taken from further on in Student A's response:

By the end of the play, Lady Macbeth is no longer a powerful woman. She has become completely broken and is mad with guilt. She tries to wash away the blood from her hands and says 'Here's the smell of blood still'. At the start of the play she thought 'A little water rids us of this deed'. Her guilty conscience has turned her into a weak character. In the end she dies and she may have committed suicide. Macbeth only comments that 'She should have died hereafter'. He doesn't seem to mind what has happened to his wife. At the end of the play she has become powerless.

In the first paragraph, Student A has shown the following skills and achievements:

- a good level of understanding of what happens in the scene
- use of four direct quotations with comments on them
- use of several direct references to the text and has used these to come to a judgement, which the question asks for
- an awareness of the audience and its possible reaction to Lady Macbeth
- starting to sustain the idea of Lady Macbeth as both evil and powerful at the end of the paragraph
- the paragraph is linked to the question.

1 Working in a pair, annotate the second paragraph of Student A's answer to see if you can find more examples of the same skills or any new ones.

2 What do you think is good about the answer?

3 Look carefully at the first three assessment objectives. What advice would you give to Student A on how to improve this answer?

Student B

This is taken from the opening of Student B's response:

The soliloquy starts with Shakespeare's use of the image of a raven. For the original audience this would have immediately suggested that something ominous was about to occur; today it means that the castle seems isolated. It is also interesting to note that Shakespeare writes 'my battlements' rather than 'our battlements'. This suggests that Lady Macbeth may consider herself to be the sole owner of the castle and that her husband is inferior to her. The audience would recognise that she considered herself to be a powerful woman with a strong sense of ownership rather than part of a partnership. Shakespeare centres the entire soliloquy about her: there is not a single mention of Macbeth, the man on whom she is relying to achieve the power she wants. The soliloquy then becomes shocking as Shakespeare explores the idea of Lady Macbeth appealing to some sort of supernatural force to stop her from being a woman when she says 'unsex me here' and 'Come to my woman's breasts, And take all my milk for gall'. In these lines Shakespeare is implying that women are nurturing and maternal and are incapable of being evil. In order to be evil, Lady Macbeth must stop being a woman. This may have shocked his audience and may still do so today, unless, of course, you consider men to be innately more powerful than women.

Annotations:

- emphasis is on Shakespeare and Lady Macbeth as a dramatic construction who does not really exist
- places idea of raven in context of Shakespeare's times
- provides alternative interpretation
- this is followed by a developed discussion of the significance of the word 'my' and what it might imply – writing a lot about a little
- not clear if this refers to original or modern audience – or both
- overview of soliloquy
- links to question
- quotations well used to illustrate point
- another link to question
- another link to question, possible interpretations of soliloquy

This is taken from further on in Student B's response:

Following this soliloquy, Shakespeare presents Lady Macbeth at work – using a venomous cocktail of emotional blackmail and insults to ensure that she gets her own way. Shakespeare returns to the image of maternal nurturing: Lady Macbeth admits that she has given birth and suckled her children but claims that she would have 'plucked her nipple from his boneless gums, And dashed the brains out' – a statement of ferocity that would shock both when first performed and now. The verb 'dashed' creates a sense of speed and force, the repeated 'd's driving the line forward to the plosive sound of 'out'. Shakespeare is emphasising that Lady Macbeth is happy to give up all sense of being a mother (and so a woman) in order to attain power.

This is a stronger response than Student A's. Student B is clearly focused on the author's craft and purpose and on the text as drama. The response engages with Shakespeare's use of language and characterisation and develops ideas about Lady Macbeth's single-minded determination to kill her way to the top. It includes personal interpretation. It shows:

- understanding of Shakespeare's characterisation of Lady Macbeth
- sustained comments on meaning of textual details
- awareness of effects on the stage and on the audience of the revelation that Lady Macbeth is utterly ruthless
- some exploration of feelings and motives
- effective use of textual detail in stage speech
- a developed consideration of Lady Macbeth as an evil, powerful woman and the ways in which some people might react differently to her.

1 In pairs, annotate the second paragraph of Student B's answer to see if you can find more examples of the same skills or any new ones.

2 What do you think is good about the answer?

3 Look carefully at the first three assessment objectives. What advice would you give to Student B on how to improve this answer?

Student C

This is taken from the opening of Student C's response:

In this soliloquy the audience is presented with a masterclass in ruthlessness. Lady Macbeth, with knowing irony, describes Duncan's imminent arrival as 'great'. She then creates a conceit of Duncan's arrival being announced not by trumpets, as would usually be the case, but rather by a raven, an omen of death to Jacobeans, whose 'croak' is 'hoarse'. Shakespeare's use of onomatopoeia and the repeated 'r' sounds produce a sinister effect. Shakespeare then presents Lady Macbeth as a powerful figure: she speaks of Duncan's 'entrance' as if he were an actor in a play she is writing. She will ensure that his fate will indeed be 'fatal'. Shakespeare shows that she is well aware of her own power when she positions Duncan's entrance as being 'under my battlements'. Duncan is given a subservient position (he is underneath rather than walking through the castle gates). The use of the first person singular shows that she believes herself to be in complete control of her castle. Macbeth is not even mentioned: he is nothing but a useful tool.

This is taken from further on in Student C's response:

That said, it is also interesting that Lady Macbeth is determined to renounce her femininity. Ambition, ruthlessness, the power to kill are shown to be masculine attributes. Shakespeare suggests that in order to achieve her desires, Lady Macbeth must stop being a woman. This is not entirely surprising for less than 20 years before Queen Elizabeth, the most powerful woman in Europe, had felt it necessary to address her troops with an admission of her fragile femininity: 'I know I have the body of a weak, feeble woman; but I have the heart and stomach of a king, and of a king of England too'. There is nothing weak and feeble about Lady Macbeth.

This is the best of the three student responses.

1 Comment on the ways in which Student C:

   a   understands what the extract is about – its ideas and its importance in the play as a whole

   b   explains the effect of the extract on an audience and shows why it has that effect

   c   uses quotations from the extract as evidence to support an argument and does not just put forward opinions without any support

   d   looks at the whole extract and does not get stuck on one part of it

   e   shows a knowledge of the context in which the play was written and how it might be received by a 21st-century audience

   f   convincingly explores and evaluates one or more of the ideas in the text as a whole.

Use your learning in this section to create practice questions and develop your skills further.

1 Work with another student to:

- choose a topic from the list in this section, or a topic of your choice
- choose a suitable extract of around 300 words
- create your practice questions.

Topics

- ambition
- loyalty
- evil
- fear
- guilt
- how good people can change
- a major character
- a minor character.

Use these prompts to create your question:

- Choose a suitable topic.
- Choose a suitable extract.
- Choose a focus for writing about the extract.

Your question should look like this:

Starting with this extract, write about how Shakespeare presents your choice of topic.

- **how Shakespeare presents your choice of focus in this extract**
- **how Shakespeare presents your choice of topic as above in the play as a whole.**

---

2 Now answer the question, using the skills you have developed.

As you plan and write, think about how you can show:

- a consistent focus on the question you have been asked, always remembering never to just retell the plot
- your knowledge of the details of the play by using direct quotations or references to the text if you cannot remember the quotations
- your understanding of a character or a setting or a theme
- your understanding of how Shakespeare has used language and structure to create the play
- your ideas about the context in which the play was written and how an audience in the 21st century might react to it.

3 Swap work with your partner. Using these points and your work in this section, comment on the skills shown in the answer. Suggest three areas that could be improved.

Glossary

adverb a word used to describe a verb or an adjective

adjective a word that describes a noun

antithesis two opposite ideas that are put together to achieve a contrasting effect

blank verse unrhymed verse with carefully placed stressed and unstressed syllables

characters the people in a story; even when based on real people, characters in a play are invented or fictionalised

characterisation the way a writer paints a picture of a particular character, through their words, actions and reactions

comedy a play that is usually light-hearted and has a happy ending

connotation an idea or a feeling linked to the main meaning of a word – what it implies or suggests in addition to its literal meaning

context the historical circumstances of a piece of writing, which affect what an author wrote and the way they wrote it; context also includes the way the writing was performed (in the case of plays such as *Macbeth*) and received by audiences.

dialogue a conversation between two or more people in a piece of writing

dramatic irony when the audience knows something about a character or plot that a character on stage is not aware of

imagery language intended to conjure up a vivid picture in the reader or audience's mind

innuendo a hint or suggestion, usually a negative one

irony directly contradicting the truth (on purpose or by accident).

juxtaposition the placement of two ideas or things near each other to invite comparison or contrast

prose writing that follows the style of normal speech.

soliloquy a long speech given by a character, usually alone on stage, as if they are thinking aloud

stage directions text in the script of a play that helps the director and actors realise in performance what the writer wanted to happen on stage to convey a particular interpretation

stereotype an oversimplified but common image or idea of a particular person or thing

stichomythia the use of short, quick alternate lines in dialogue between two characters

supernatural something that cannot be explained by the known laws of science and nature

theme an idea or concept that recurs throughout a play

tragedy a play with an unhappy ending, usually involving the downfall of the main character

verse writing that has a particular rhyme, pattern or rhythm

Acknowledgements

Picture credits

p. 4 Donald Cooper/Photostage; p. 7 Geraint Lewis; p. 8 Donald Cooper/Photostage; p. 12 Donald Cooper/Photostage; p. 14 Donald Cooper/Photostage; p. 15 Johan Persson/ArenaPAL/Topfoto; p. 16 Donald Cooper/Photostage; p. 20 Donald Cooper/Photostage; p. 22 Donald Cooper/Photostage; p. 24 Donald Cooper/Photostage; p. 25 Dominic Dibbs/Topfoto; p. 26 Donald Cooper/Photostage; p. 27 Fritz Curzon/ArenaPAL/Topfoto; p. 28 Clive Barda/ArenaPAL; p. 29 Donald Cooper/Photostage; p. 30 Donald Cooper/Photostage; p. 31 Donald Cooper/Photostage; p. 33 Donald Cooper/Photostage; p. 35 Donald Cooper/Photostage; p. 36 Donald Cooper/Photostage; p. 37 Donald Cooper/Photostage; p. 38 Donald Cooper/Photostage; p. 39 Donald Cooper/Photostage; p. 40 Donald Cooper/Photostage; p. 42 Johan Persson/ArenaPAL/Topfoto; p. 43 Donald Cooper/Photostage; p. 45 Donald Cooper/Photostage; p. 47 Johan Persson/ArenaPAL/Topfoto; p. 48 Donald Cooper/Photostage; p. 50 Donald Cooper/Photostage; p. 51 Geraint Lewis; p. 52 Geraint Lewis; p. 53 Donald Cooper/Photostage; p. 54 Elliott Franks/ArenaPAL/Topfoto; p. 55 Donald Cooper/Photostage; p. 57 Donald Cooper/Photostage; p. 59 Donald Cooper/Photostage; p. 60 Donald Cooper/Photostage; p. 61 Donald Cooper/Photostage; p. 62 Donald Cooper/Photostage; p. 63 Johan Persson/ArenaPAL/Topfoto; p. 64 Donald Cooper/Photostage; p. 66 Johan Persson/ArenaPAL/Topfoto; p. 68 Donald Cooper/Photostage; p. 70 Donald Cooper/Photostage; p. 72 Johan Persson/ArenaPAL/Topfoto; p. 73 Donald Cooper/Photostage; p. 74 Donald Cooper/Photostage; p. 75 Donald Cooper/Photostage; p. 77 hellena13/Thinkstock; p. 78 Donald Cooper/Photostage; p. 79 Johan Persson/ArenaPAL/Topfoto; p. 81 Donald Cooper/Photostage; p. 82 Donald Cooper/Photostage; p. 83 Johan Persson/ArenaPAL/Topfoto; p. 84 Donald Cooper/Photostage; p. 86 Donald Cooper/Photostage; p. 87 Donald Cooper/Photostage; p. 88 Pete Jones/ArenaPAL/Topfoto; p. 89 Donald Cooper/Photostage; p. 91 Clive Barda/ArenaPAL/Topfoto; p. 93 Johan Persson/ArenaPAL/Topfoto; p. 94 Donald Cooper/Photostage.

Produced for Cambridge University Press by

White-Thomson Publishing
www.wtpub.co.uk
Managing editor: Sonya Newland
Designer: Kevin Knight